Crowning Glory
The Merits of Monarchy

CROWNING GLORY

The Merits of Monarchy

Charles Neilson Gattey

SHEPHEARD-WALWYN

First published in 2002 by
Shepheard-Walwyn (Publishers) Ltd
Suite 604, The Chandlery
50 Westminster Bridge Road
London SE1 7QY

British Library Cataloguing in Publication Data
A catalogue record of this book
is available from the British Library

ISBN 0 85683 196 4

Typeset by R E Clayton
Printed in Great Britain by Bookcraft (CPI Group),
Midsomer Norton

Contents

Acknowledgements

The author and publisher wish to thank the following for giving permission to reproduce their copyright material as illustrations in the book and on the jacket:

On the jacket – Beaton/Camera Press

Illustrations 1-6, 8-10 and 12-13 – Retrograph Archive

Illustrations 7, 11 and 14-16 – Hulton Archive

List of Illustrations

Introduction

"**B**y the end of this century, there will be only five Kings left – those of Hearts, Diamonds, Spades, Clubs, and England," King Farouk predicted in 1951, according to his biographer Michael Stern. The only time Kings and Queens in packs of cards were abolished was in France during the Revolution when they were replaced by Citizens and Citizenesses – but it made playing cards games so boring that nobody used the new packs.

However, Farouk had good cause for making such a prediction. His overthrow was then the latest in a long line since the Russian Revolution and the rise of Socialism and Communism had swept away not only the Russian Imperial Family, but also the dynasties of Austria-Hungary, Germany, Turkey, Spain and Portugal following the First World War, and, after the Second, Italy and a number of East European kingdoms. The contagion was spreading to the Middle East with revolutions in Iraq and Egypt – the tide seemed unstoppable. Other kingdoms were to topple after his, those in Libya, Burma, Laos and Cambodia.

Farouk's prediction about England proved correct, but the five most stable countries in Europe also retained their monarchs. Moreover, in Spain the restoration of the monarchy was part of the means of re-introducing democracy, and King Juan Carlos later defended democracy against an attempted army coup. He has also added to his popularity by running and financing one of the world's most successful and admired soccer squads, *Real Madrid*. In other countries now, monarchy is being considered as a way of healing past division: most recently in Afghanistan, but also in Eastern Europe, King Simeon of Bulgaria has returned to his country and the Crown Prince of Yugoslavia has been allowed back and had some of his property restored. Nevertheless, it is interesting that Farouk recognised something special about the British monarchy. Perhaps it was as a result of having had an English governess as a boy.

The traditional customs connected with the British monarchy certainly bring colour and elegance into the monotonous ugliness of a machine-ridden age. Britain's royal occasions are the envy of other nations for in themselves they symbolise the perfection of performance which most civilized people crave. The buildings and regalia associated with past Kings and Queens form one of the chief tourist attractions which bring millions of pounds' worth of foreign currencies that are spent here.

While the monarchy is mainly a conservative force, helping to maintain stability, this very fundamental stability enables the country to absorb more radical changes in its political and social structure than would otherwise be possible without risk of disorder. To quote the late Malcolm Muggeridge: "Monarchy is the bridge between what is fluctuating and what is everlasting in human affairs."

"The evil men do lives after them, the good is oft interred with their bones," said Mark Anthony of Julius Caesar. We remember Henry VIII's cruelty and Charles II's mistresses but ignore their merits. Let me begin with a King about whom only good (except that he burnt some cakes) is known, which may explain why he is forgotten in our cynical age.

Alfred the Great delivered England from the Danes. He was a scholar and an author – in fact the father of English prose – for before him only verse had been written in our native tongue. He was an educator of his people. He codified the laws and enforced them. He built up the English navy from a tiny beginning.

Few know anything about King Canute except that he got his feet wet trying vainly to command the tide – a travesty of the facts. He was King of England by conquest before he was 20, and when he died aged 40 most of northern Europe lay under his rule and at peace, for he genuinely desired it and brought it to all the people he protected. He was the creator of the first United States of Europe. Under his new code of laws both the rich and the poor became for the first time equal, and the practice of condemning people to death for trivial offences ended, so did all forms of slavery. The coinage was reformed in England. It disturbed him that many of his people began to worship him as a God. He decided that he must destroy this belief by publicly demonstrating that he was as human as they were and that was why he staged the incident of attempting to command the tide. When he failed, he took off his crown and had it placed upon the great cross in the Minster at Winchester as a token of his humility. Never again did he wear it.

William the Conqueror, despite his ruthlessness, was a just and far-sighted ruler, and there was little lawlessness in his reign. He caused the Domesday Book to be compiled and created the New Forest which, had he not, might today be instead a concrete jungle.

Henry II introduced a system of common law to the whole kingdom, in place of the various provincial customs administered in the shires and hundreds and in the innumerable private jurisdictions. He commenced the new procedure of trial by jury, instead of the old barbarous method of trial by compurgation, ordeal by hot iron or battle with one's adversary.

Edward I has been called the English Justinian. The first eighteen years of his reign saw the beginning of our statute law. The legally minded King passed statute after statute through his Parliaments which changed the very substance of the law. Hitherto it had been traditional and unwritten. His first statutes remained so long the basis of our law of real property that a knowledge of them became essential for all English lawyers up until our day. He founded Westminster School, whose *alumni* of distinction include Ben Jonson, Dryden, George Herbert, William Cowper, Sir Christopher Wren and Edward Gibbon.

Edward III founded the Order of the Garter to signal the triumph of chastity over temptation. He brought over many Flemings who laid the foundations of our textile industry, and was also the first monarch to appoint Justices of the Peace.

Cambridge University was probably founded in the reign of Henry III. In 1229 he offered asylum to scholars exiled from Paris. Two years later he told the Mayor, who was objecting to this, that scholars from abroad brought honour and profit to England and that they should be pleased to accept them.

Henry VI was a great patron of learning. He founded four university colleges and Eton – originally for poor scholars who could not pay for their schooling. His successor Edward IV began Windsor's beautiful St. George's Chapel which was completed by Henry VIII. He was the friend and patron of William Caxton and his book collection became the nucleus of the old Royal Library and later one of the treasures of the British Library.

The jewel of Westminster Abbey is the magnificent Chapel built by Henry VII whose victory at Bosworth Field brought peace after the havoc caused to the country by the Wars of the Roses. He curbed the power of the nobles and worked hard to revive the country's lost maritime prosperity. He financed John Cabot on his voyages of exploration to Newfoundland and Nova Scotia, the practical result of which was our exploitation of the Newfoundland fishery.

Henry VIII worked hard to build up the English navy that had almost vanished during the Wars of the Roses. He was ever ready to experiment. Guns increased in range and power and Englishmen rapidly became as skilful as gunners as they were as archers in the Middle Ages. When he ascended the throne, there were only seven ships in the Royal Navy and, when he died, that number had grown to fifty-three. Henry was also a gifted musician and his composition '*Greensleeves*' has become part of our musical heritage. We owe to him many of our most attractive historical buildings: Hampton Court which he took from Wolsey and then embellished, and the handsome gate tower with its ornate clock which is the most attractive feature of St. James's Palace.

Elizabeth I had, it was said, a heart that was cold, but it was a heart of oak. She came to the throne of a country in despair and left it prosperous, rich in a renaissance of all the arts. It was also said that she loved nothing and nobody but England.

Charles I was the most outstanding art connoisseur of his time – patron of Velasquez, Bernini and Van Dyck. He amassed the most valuable collection of Renaissance paintings ever assembled in England. Most were sold abroad by Cromwell but a few survived to form the nucleus of the finest royal art collection in the world today.

Under Oliver Cromwell's Puritan Republican régime all theatres were closed. We owe it to Charles II that they were reopened and that the brilliant comedies of manners of Wycherley were staged. In the great dining-room of Christ's Hospital hangs a painting by Verrio which occupies most of the wall: it depicts a scene at the court of the Merry Monarch but no debauched courtiers are to be seen only grave men of learning, and in the foreground before the throne are girls and boys of the school. The latter are in blue coats and yellow stockings, the Tudor costume of 1552 when it was founded by Edward VI to educate poor children. The picture was painted to commemorate the foundation of the royal mathematical school at Christ's Hospital by Charles II.

The Merry Monarch was also a great patron of other arts. He founded the office of Master of the King's Musick, had an expert knowledge of architecture, supervised in person alterations and improvements to royal palaces. He had, too, a passion for gardening, recreating St. James's Park, planting flowers and walks of trees which are still there today. He also planted Love Walk, that beautiful avenue of trees going from Windsor Castle to the Great Park – and laid out Greenwich Park. To him we owe the Theatre Royal in Drury Lane and what is today the world's most prestigious scientific body, the Royal Society.

With the King's active encouragement men such as Isaac Newton, Robert Boyle, Edward Halley and Robert Hooke discovered many of the principles which are fundamental to modern astronomy, chemistry and physics. Charles conducted his own experiments in a laboratory at Whitehall Palace. He founded Greenwich Laboratory and it is from its meridian that longitude is reckoned.

Charles II with his brother the Duke of York, later King James II, rendered sterling services to Londoners during the Great Fire of London. Insensible to peril they rode through the city all day long calming the populace. Ankle-deep in water for many hours altogether, they handled buckets with as much diligence as the poorest man, thus maintaining morale. The famous Royal Hospital at Chelsea, home of the soldier pensioners, built by Wren, owes its existence to Charles whose statue by Grinling Gibbons stands in the centre of the front quadrangle.

If the Restoration had not taken place, Hyde Park today would be covered with houses and offices like the rest of its surroundings. It had been a forest in Henry VIII's times. He used it for hunting but James I opened it to the public. Oliver Cromwell sold it to speculators for building, but fortunately he died before this could take place and it was restored to the Crown.

That bathing haven in sweltering summers, the Serpentine, owes its existence to Queen Caroline, George II's wife, who had it prepared in 1730 at royal expense. Later, on account of the numerous accidents which had been occurring there, George III in 1794 gave a plot on the ground of the northern bank so that the Royal Humane Society might erect a house for the rendering of first aid to drowning persons.

George II's patronage of music led to a remarkable demonstration of loyalty when the Jacobite Rebellion seemed like succeeding. On 28th September 1745 a week after Cope's army was routed at Prestonpans, an arrangement Dr. Arne had specially prepared of the old English tune of 'God Save Our Noble Queen' was sung as an anthem on Drury Lane's stage and encored. Arne's pupil, Charles Burney, then made his own version for Covent Garden where it was greeted with similar fervour and continued to be sung every night until the rising was crushed. It was in this fashion that 'God Save The King' gained its place as the anthem for both Sovereign and State.

It was George II who in 1757 gave the Royal Library to the British Museum which brought with it the privilege of compulsory deposit with the library of all newly published books which still holds good.

His grandson George III fostered agricultural development and founded model farms and gave Crown lands to the nation in 1761 in return for a fixed income. They are worth a thousand times more today than then, so the nation has benefited hugely.

George IV is perhaps best remembered as far as buildings are concerned by the Marine Pavilion at Brighton. In a generation trained to admire classical simplicity, its pagodas, minarets, oriental domes were derided, but today it is the chief glory of Brighton which by his patronage he made popular.

It was George, who as Prince Regent, engaged Nash against considerable opposition as the architect for the redevelopment scheme that was to transform the face of central London. Marylebone Park – an expanse of open land north of Portland Place had just reverted to the Crown from the noble families to whom it had been let. The development was to be known as Regent's Park – the road that led to it as Regent's Street. These impressive improvements of London would never have taken place without the Prince Regent's advocacy. They were severely criticised at the time. Nash's architecture was called meretricious and monstrous. Only the Regent had the imagination and the artistic taste to foresee how delightful Nash's project would turn out to be when completed.

Windsor Castle was in a sorry state and turning into a ruin in parts. George IV engaged Wyatville to restore and remodel it. The round tower was raised by a stone crown 30 feet higher than the former structure. The new Grand Corridor, 550 feet in length, provided a magnificent picture gallery as well as a covered way between the north front and the east. Some were upset by the changes, but most, including Sir Walter Scott, thought that the result was successful and impressive. An essentially Gothic structure demanded Gothic treatment and Wyatville turned Windsor Castle into one of most distinctive Gothic monuments in the world.

Another now admired cultural treasure, the marble friezes from the neglected Parthenon brought back from Greece by the Earl of Elgin, were bought for the British Museum thanks to the Prince Regent's active support and despite criticism from self-styled experts.

George was extremely humane. One of his first acts as King was to abolish the legal use of torture in his Kingdom of Hanover and the flogging of female prisoners. He was always urging his Ministers to lessen the severity of legal punishment. He also did all he could to protect animals from cruelty and was a personal friend of Richard Martin M.P. – responsible for the first legislation anywhere in the world for the prevention of cruelty to animals – and helped to found the Royal Society for the Prevention of Cruelty to Animals.

The First Gentleman in Europe, as George was dubbed, had only to hear of an actor or indeed anyone in distress and he would send them money. He regularly supported numerous charities from foundling hospitals to old people's homes, from the British and Foreign Schools Society to the Royal Infirmary for Diseases of the Eye. Even his adversary, Henry Brougham, praised him for his staunch and generous support of popular education. He presented his father's library of more than 65,000 volumes to the British Museum – gave the Royal Academy casts of notable ancient statues specially copied at his expense in Italy – paid for a new quadrangle at Trinity College – and contributed towards the upkeep of English students in Rome, etc.

A project dear to George IV's heart was the formation of a national treasury of pictures to rival any in the world. He succeeded in restoring the Royal Collection to the eminent position it had held before the Puritan art-haters of the Commonwealth Government had sold off abroad for practically nothing the superb paintings purchased by Charles I. George was always happy for the public to see his own collection. "I have not formed it for my pleasure alone," he commented when lending his Carlton House paintings for an exhibition in 1826. "I wanted them as well to gratify the public taste." In 1814 he bought 86 splendid pictures from Sir Thomas Baring – in 1819 he bought Rubens' *Farm at Laeken* at a sale in Paris and also that year Rembrandt's *Lady with a Fan*, a superb companion for the same painter's *Shipbuilder and His Wife* which he had acquired at Christie's some years before with fine paintings by Adraen Van Velde, Wouwermans and Ostades. He bought Mieris's *Fruiterer's Shop* – etc.

But George IV did not confine his purchases to Old Masters. He was always encouraging contemporary British artists, placing year by year more and more commissions for portraits of his family, friends, distinguished contemporaries, and his animals.

He patronised sculptors, too – John Flaxman, Richard Westmacott, Chantrey. The National Gallery came into existence as a result of the government's accepting his advice to start a National Collection by buying the 38 pictures in the Angerstein Collection in 1823 as a nucleus.

George IV's successor was his brother, William IV, who had the delicate task of coping with the passions surrounding the passing of the Reform Bill of 1832 which enfranchised the middle class. He was personally popular and known to favour change. He, and especially his wife, Queen Adelaide, contributed large sums to good causes, creating goodwill in turbulent times which had seen several revolutions in Europe and the accession of the 'Citizen King', Louise Philippe, in France.

Queen Victoria and
Her Prince Consort

When Queen Victoria succeeded her uncle on 20th June 1837, she was only eighteen. She was initially very much under the influence of the Prime Minister, Lord Melbourne, and the Whigs, but her reign marks a significant change in the role of the monarchy. With her husband's advice and support, she raised the monarchy above party politics, creating the role of the constitutional monarch. Walter Bagehot commenting on this in his book *The English Constitution*, published in 1867, noted that it was first during her reign that the concept of the constitutional monarch and the person suited to play that role emerged. Thanks to her skill, the power of the monarchy having waned, its influence increased and she remained securely on the throne during 1848, the next year of revolution in Europe. Showing remarkable fortitude during her long reign, she displayed what Lord Salisbury described as an "inborn and inextinguishable consciousness of Queen-ship".

Vernon Bogdanor, Professor of Government at Oxford University, wrote in 1995 in his perceptive book, *The Monarchy and the Constitution*, that Queen Victoria showed that the decline in power could be replaced by influence. But there was no easy route to this. As Bagehot had stressed, the details of political affairs were "vast, disagreeable, complicated and miscellaneous". A monarch to be the equal of his ministers in discussion must work as they work.

Professor Bogdanor writes that Victoria was the first sovereign to master the endless boxes of state papers sent to her with such monotonous regularity by her private secretary.

It has been said that no monarch in history wrote so much and few as well as Queen Victoria. She started keeping a diary at the age of thirteen which she later called her *Journal* and this continued unbroken in fascinating detail until her death nearly seventy years later. Her average daily output as an adult was about 2,500 words, all now preserved in the Royal Archives. This reached a total of some sixty million in the course of her reign. Had she been a novelist, her complete works would have run into seven hundred volumes, published at the rate of one a month. She wrote in a forthright, trenchant style. They reflect the development of her character from the shy young Queen whom her first Prime Minister, Lord Melbourne, loved as he might protectively have loved as his own daughter, to the formidable old lady of whom even Bismarck stood in awe. An author asked if he could present her with a copy of his book against vivisection. The reply was: "The Queen will readily accept it. The subject causes her whole nature to boil over against these 'butchers'."

One of the more positive sides of Queen Victoria's upbringing was that she was encouraged to help those in need. In 1836, she took a great interest in a gypsy family which her mother had helped, and wrote in her *Journal* for Christmas Day that she had been worrying to think that they might perish on account of the bitter weather, so she had taken steps to see that they were provided with nourishing food, warm clothing and bedding. She worried, too, about the widows and orphans of the Hartley Colliery disaster and the slaves in Africa and wished she could help them. Being the least vain of any of her royal contemporaries, after the Prince Consort's death she did her best to see that no photographs of her were in any way touched up and showed her as a plain ageing woman.

Victoria wrote in her *Journal* for 20th June 1837 that her mother had awoken her at six o'clock in the morning to say that the Archbishop of Canterbury and the Lord Chamberlain had arrived and wanted to see her. The 18-year old girl went into her sitting-room alone wearing a dressing-gown. She learnt that her uncle, King William IV, had died just after midnight and that she was now Queen. Later, that morning, she wrote in her *Journal*: "Since it has pleased Providence to place me in this station, I shall do my utmost to fulfil my duty towards my country. I am very young and perhaps in many, though not in all, things inexperienced, but I am sure, that very few have more real good will and more desire to do what is fit and right than I have."

During breakfast, "good faithful" Baron Stockmar (who had been sent to England by Victoria's uncle, King Leopold of the Belgians, to advise her) arrived. She then wrote a letter to Leopold. One was delivered to her from the Prime Minister, Lord Melbourne, to say that he would call at nine. She saw him in her room quite alone as she always now did with all her Ministers. "He kissed my hand and I then acquainted him that it had long been my intention to retain him and the rest of the present Ministry at the head of affairs, and that it could not be in better hands than his. He then handed to me the Declaration which I was to read to the Council. I talked with him some little time longer after which he left me. I like him very much and feel confidence in him. He is a very straightforward, honest, clever and good man... At about ½ p. 11, I held a Council in the red saloon... Took my dinner upstairs alone. At about 20 minutes to 9 Lord Melbourne returned and remained till near 10. I had a very important and a very comfortable conversation with him. Each time I see him I feel more confidence in him."

Next, on 24th June, Victoria mentioned in her *Journal*: "I receive so many communications now from my Ministers, but I like it very much."

In July, Queen Victoria drove to the House of Lords for the prorogation of Parliament and wrote on the 17th that, wearing her Robe which was very heavy, she entered the House with Melbourne bearing the Sword of State walking just before her. "I felt somewhat nervous before I read my speech, but it went very well, and I was happy to hear people were satisfied."

On 28th September, Victoria wrote that she had reviewed a parade of Guardsmen and Lancers in Windsor Great Park. "I saluted them by putting my hand to my cap like the officers do, and was much admired for my manner of doing so. I then cantered back to my first position and there remained as the Troops marched by in slow and quick time, and when they manoeuvred, which they did beautifully, I felt for the first time like a man, as if I could fight myself at the head of my troops. I am very sorry indeed to go from Windsor. I passed such a very pleasant time here; the pleasantest summer I ever passed in my life, and I shall never forget the first summer of my Reign."

On 9th November that year, the young Queen wrote a long account in her *Journal* of the first Lord Mayor of London's dinner she attended at the Guildhall. Throughout her progress in the state carriage to the City, she had met "with the most gratifying, affectionate, hearty and brilliant reception from the greatest concourse of people I ever witnessed". She felt deeply grateful. "It is much more than I deserve, and I shall do my utmost to render myself worthy of all this love."

On the 17th November Victoria wrote about a visit after dinner to the play at Covent Garden. "I met with the same brilliant reception, the house being so full that many people had to be pulled out of the Pit by their wrists and arms into the Dress Circle. I never saw such an exhibition; my Ladies took it by turns, (their standing behind me, I mean)."

On 28th June, the following year, Victoria was crowned, and afterwards she wrote a long account in her *Journal*: "It was a fine day and the crowds exceeded what I had ever seen. The Bishop of Durham stood on the side near me, but he was, as Lord Melbourne warned me, remarkably *maladroit* and could never tell me what was to take place."

Charles Greville wrote later in his *Journal* that 87-years old Lord Rolle fell down as he was climbing the steps to pay homage to the Queen. Her first impulse was to rise, and when afterwards he came again, she said: "May I not get up and meet him?" Then she rose from the throne and advanced down two steps to prevent him coming up, an act of graciousness that caused a great sensation.

When they went into St Edward's Chapel it looked, as Lord Melbourne said later, more unlike a Chapel than anything he had ever seen, for what was called an altar was covered with sandwiches, bottles of wine, etc., etc. Victoria wrote: "The Archbishop came in and ought to have delivered the Orb to me, but I had already got it, and he (as usual) was so confused and puzzled and knew nothing – and went away. Here we waited some minutes. Lord Melbourne took a glass of wine, for he seemed completely tired. The Procession being formed I replaced my Crown (which I had taken off for a few minutes) took the Orb in my left hand and the Sceptre in my right, and thus loaded proceeded through the Abbey, which resounded with cheers, to the first robing-room. And here we waited for at least an hour. The Archbishop had (most awkwardly) put the ring on the wrong finger, and the consequence was that I had the greatest difficulty in getting it off again, which at last I did with great pain. At about half-past four I re-entered my carriage, the Crown on my head, and the Sceptre and Orb in my hands, and we proceeded the same way as we came – the crowds, if possible, having increased. The enthusiasm, affection and loyalty were really touching, and I shall ever remember this day as the proudest of my life. I came home at a little after six, really not feeling tired."

The Coronation over, the Government became concerned as to whom Victoria should marry. It was decided that the most suitable persons were her cousins, Ernest and Albert, and so on 10th October 1839 they arrived as guests at Windsor Castle. Next day the Queen wrote in her *Journal*: "Albert is so extremely handsome – such beautiful blue eyes, an exquisite nose, and such a pretty mouth with delicate moustachios and slight but very slight whiskers, a beautiful figure, broad in the shoulders and a fine waist... It is quite a pleasure to look at Albert when he gallops and valses, he does it beautifully and holds himself so well."

On the 13th Victoria wrote that seeing her two cousins had changed her opinion as to marrying and that she must decide soon which was a difficult thing. "You should take another week," advised Lord Melbourne.

Victoria readily agreed and said that Albert was so amiable and good-tempered as well, whilst she had such a bad temper. Next day, Victoria wrote: "After a little pause I said to Lord Melbourne that I had made up my mind about marrying dearest Albert. 'You have?' he said. 'Well then, about the time?' Not for a year, I thought, which he said was too long. That Parliament must be assembled in order to make a provision for him, and that if it was settled, it shouldn't be talked about. 'It prevents any objections, though I don't think there'll be much.' Then I asked if I hadn't better tell Albert of my decision soon, in which Lord M. agreed. 'How?' I asked for that in general such things were done the other way – which made Lord M. laugh."

At about half past midday on the 15th, Victoria sent for Albert and told him it would make her very happy if he would consent to marry her. "We embraced each other over and over again, and he was so kind, so affectionate."

Victoria had planned that her honeymoon should consist of two or three days spent in Windsor Castle which disappointed Albert and he told her so. On 31st January she wrote to him: "You have forgotten, my dearest love, that I am the Sovereign, and that business can stop and wait for nothing. Parliament is sitting, and something occurs almost every day, for which I may be required, and it is quite impossible for me to be absent from London; therefore two or three days is already a long time to be absent. I am never easy a moment if I am not on the spot, and see and hear what is going on, and everybody, including all my aunts (who are very knowing in all these things), say I must come out after the second day, for, as I must be surrounded by my Court, I cannot keep alone. This is also my own wish in every way."

On the morning of the wedding, which took place on 10th February in the Chapel Royal, St James's, Victoria sent a note by hand to Albert: "How are you today, and have you slept well? I have rested very well, and feel very comfortable today. What weather! I believe, however, the rain will cease. Send one word when you, my most dearly loved bridegroom, will be ready. Thy ever-faithful, Victoria R."

In her *Journal*, the bride wrote at length. She had risen at a quarter to nine, having slept well. She had seen Albert for the last time as her bridegroom. At a quarter to twelve she set off. After the marriage ceremony, they returned to the Palace for the wedding breakfast. At about four o'clock, she and Albert drove to Windsor Castle where he took her on his knee and kissed her "and was so dear and kind". They dined in her sitting-room. "He called me names of tenderness, I have never yet heard used to me before – bliss beyond belief! May God help me to do my duty as I ought and be worthy of such blessings."

Next, Victoria wrote: "When day dawned (for we did not sleep much) and I beheld that beautiful angelic face by my side, it was more than I can express! We got up at a quarter past eight. When I had laced, I went to dearest Albert's room, and we breakfasted together."

On the 13th, Victoria recorded: "My dearest Albert put on my stockings for me. I went in and saw him shave, a great delight."

Three days later, Victoria wrote to her obedient bridegroom: "I always think that it is safer to write in English, as I try to be very legible. I am much grieved that you feel disappointed about my wish respecting your gentlemen, but very glad that you consent to it, and that you feel confidence in my choice."

The Queen wrote in her *Journal* on the same day of that year that she had talked to Lord Melbourne about Albert's fear of their not putting people of good character about him and the former had replied that the wife of Lord John Russell (then Secretary for War) had said: "The Prince's character is such as is highly approved at a German university, but would be subject to ridicule at ours." Victoria continued that Melbourne himself had remarked on another occasion that any attention to morality in universities was ridiculed. This had shocked her, and she had asked whether this meant he didn't like Albert so much as he would if he were not so strict. " 'Oh! No, I highly respect it,' had said Lord M. I then talked of Albert's saying I ought to be severe about people. 'Then you'll be liable to make every sort of mistake. In this country all should go by law and precedent,' said Lord M., 'and not by what you hear.' "

On 24th January, Lord John Russell proposed an allowance of £50,000 a year for Prince Albert. A motion put forward by the Radical, Joseph Hume, to reduce this annuity to £21,000 was defeated. But, on 27th January, a Tory M.P., supported by Sir Robert Peel, proposed £30,000, which was carried to the Queen's disgust, as she thought even £50,000 was insufficient.

Prince Albert had expected to be allowed to choose for himself those in his household, but Victoria wrote to him on 8th December: "I must tell you quite honestly that it will not do. You may rely upon my care that you shall have proper people, and not idle and too young, and Lord Melbourne has already mentioned several to me who would be very suitable."

Albert protested in vain against his having to take the Prime Minister's Secretary as his own. Would this not make him a partisan in the eyes of many? "Think of my position, dear Victoria," he pleaded. "I am leaving my home with all its old associations, all my bosom friends, and going to a country in which everything is new and strange to me... Is it not to be conceded that the two or three persons who are to have charge of my private affairs should be persons who already have my confidence?"

The bride-to-be replied on 23rd December, underlining almost every word: "It is, as you rightly suppose, my greatest, my most anxious wish to do everything most agreeable to you... Though I am very anxious you should not appear to belong to a Party, still it is necessary that your household should not form a too strong contrast to mine, else they will say: 'Oh, we know the Prince says he belongs to no party, but we are sure he is a Tory!' Therefore it is also necessary that it should appear that you went with me in having some of your people who are staunch Whigs... Do not think because I urge this, Lord M. prefers it; on the contrary, he never urged it, and I only do it as I know it is for your own good. You will pardon this long story. It will also not do to wait till you come to appoint all your people. I am distressed to tell you what I fear you do not like, but it is necessary, my dearest, most excellent Albert. Once more I tell you that you can perfectly rely on me in these matters."

At the start of the marriage, Victoria strictly refused to allow Albert to have anything to do with matters of state except, as she put it, "help with the blotting paper". It was not long, however, before the Prince, as Christopher Hibbert writes: "patient, forbearing and persuasive as well as shrewd, had assumed that benign yet overwhelming influence that was to last beyond his death."

When Prince Albert laid the foundation stone of the new Royal Exchange on 17ᵗʰ January 1842 Victoria wrote next day to her cousin, King Leopold, that "he always fascinates the people wherever he goes, by his very modest and unostentatious yet dignified ways".

In September 1842, Queen Victoria wrote to Lord Melbourne after her first visit as well as Prince Albert's to the Scottish Highlands that they both found them so beautiful that they were most anxious to return there. She added: "We greatly admired Edinburgh; the situation as well as the town is most striking; and the Prince, who also has seen so much, says it is the finest town he ever saw!" Three years later, the Queen bought the lease of Balmoral Castle, and after receiving a large and unexpected bequest from an eccentric miser, purchased the entire estate of some 17,000 acres. Finding the house itself too small, a new one was built to Prince Albert's designs.

On 28ᵗʰ September 1853, the sun shone brightly for the ceremony of laying the foundation stone of the new house. By 13ᵗʰ October 1856, the delighted Queen was able to write: "Every year my heart becomes more fixed in this dear Paradise, and so much more so, that all has become my dearest Albert's own creation, own work, own building, own laying-out, as at Osborne; and his great taste, and the impress of his dear hand, have been stamped everywhere. He was very busy today, settling and arranging many things for next year."

In the 1850s, Prince Albert initiated a survey of the entire collection of pictures in Queen Victoria's possession. He also himself began sorting and arranging the superb collection of 15,000 Old Master drawings and engravings kept in Windsor Castle's Print Room. He classified them according to artist and subject. He and the Queen added modern artists' works and started collecting miniatures to support those already in royal keeping.

The Queen wrote later: "In this, as in everything else, his great unselfish mind showed itself. He would have nothing kept for himself – but placed all in the Royal Collection saying: 'I see them just as often, and I know they are safe and cannot be lost, whereas if they were carried about in boxes or left in drawers – they were forgotten and might be lost or injured.' How true, how wise! All for futurity and for the general good – nothing for himself and he enjoyed it much more if it was for others."

One winter, Victoria wrote a very full account of her daily life at Buckingham Palace with her husband. At about 8 a.m., he would go into her bedroom to tell her it was time to rise, bring her in his letters that were in English to read through. "Also drafts of answers and letters to the Ministers (all of which are preserved in those invaluable books of political and family events which he compiled so beautifully)... Formerly, he used to be ready frequently before me... and he would either stop in my sitting-room next door to read some of the endless numbers of despatches which I placed on his table, having either read them or looked into them before... He never went out or came home without coming thro' my room or into my dressing-room – dear, dear Angel with a smile on his dearest beautiful face – and I treasured up every-thing I heard, kept every letter in a box to tell and show him, and was always so vexed and nervous if I had any foolish draft or despatch to show him, as I knew it would distress and irritate him... At breakfast and luncheon and also at our family dinners he sat at the top of table and enlivened the meals thanks to his interesting conversation... The younger children he kept in order if they ate badly... A word from him was instantly obeyed."

Prince Albert was intensely interested in modern inventions. Speaking at the Mansion House on 21st March 1850, he said: "Modern inventions will lead to the uniting of all mankind. Science and art are the guiding factors. Science discovers laws which are then applied by industry, and art gives form according to the laws of beauty and symmetry, to what is produced. In this context I believe it is the duty of every educated person to watch and study the time in which he lives, and, as far as in him lies, to add his humble mite of individual exertion to further the accomplishment of what he believes Providence to have ordained."

The Prince held that working people should not regard themselves as slaves but should be encouraged to take a pride in their work by being taught to understand the principle and ingenuity of the machines among which their lives were spent. Once this understanding had been gained, they should be given the chance of broadening this knowledge still further. This was the principle behind the Prince's plans for the *Museum of Science and Art* at South Kensington where the working classes would have an equal chance with the rich to see for themselves what science and art had achieved.

It was inevitable that photography, a nineteenth century invention which combined techniques of science and art should claim Prince Albert's attention. His attitude to it was broadly two-fold. He saw it as an art form (and therefore a potential method of instruction) and also as a recording system.

Prince Albert was committed to improving the lot of the British working classes. He felt that was one of the ways in which he could refute the accusation that he was paid £30,000 annually "for doing nothing". When the Queen became patron of a Ball in aid of unemployed Spitalfields weavers and ordered court ladies to wear only British-made clothes in her drawing-rooms, he commented: "There must be some better way of helping the poor." As a result, she invited Lord Shaftesbury to Osborne to advise her on the best ways of showing her interest in helping them. Shaftesbury thought that the Prince should put himself at the head of all social movements in art and science – "and especially of those movements as they bear upon the poor, and thus show the interest felt by Royalty in the happiness of the Kingdom".

Shaftesbury suggested that Prince Albert should visit a slum and then take the chair at a meeting in Exeter Hall of the Society for Improving the Condition of the Labouring Classes. Ignoring the disapproval of the Prime Minister and the Home Secretary, the Prince did this, having previously rehearsed his speech with the Queen. It was later published in full. He told the gathering that the interests of classes too often contrasted were identical, and that it was only ignorance which prevented their uniting for each other's advantage. Lord Shaftesbury declared: "Rank, leisure, station are gifts of God, for which man must give an account. Here is a full-proof, a glowing instance!" A worried Republican grumbled: "If the Prince goes on like this, he'll upset our apple cart."

In a letter to Charles Phipps, his Private Secretary, in 1849, Albert listed ways in which he believed the lives of the working-classes could be bettered: children should receive sympathetic industrial training, comfortable homes; in the country they should live in cottages with allotments adjacent. Their use of Savings Banks should be encouraged as well as of benefit societies, ideally run by workers themselves. At his own expense, he paid to have a pair of cottages designed by him on display in the 1851 Great Exhibition with the aim of getting developers and manufacturers to follow his lead.

To prove that he meant the monarchy to help in practical ways, Albert formulated new guidelines for his Privy Purse. Money was raised for good causes through charity dinners and garden parties. He concentrated attention on thus recovering support for the Monarchy where Chartism was strongest, organising royal tours to such areas. Foundation stones were laid by the Queen or himself for buildings intended to be used by the working-classes. Albert paid a special visit to Thomas Bazley's factory in Bolton and was delighted to find that most of his earlier proposals had been put into being. On the route from Salford to Manchester, according to eye-witnesses, a million people lined the route which pleased the Queen, who had already said of her husband's civic work: "I glory in his being seen and loved."

In her speech to Parliament on 31st January 1850, Victoria told them: "By combining liberty with order, by preserving what is valuable and amending what is defective, you will sustain the fabric of our institutions as the shelter of a free and happy people."

Prince Albert was actively interested in all sides of army organisation. In the early 1850s nowhere in England was there a camp for the training of large numbers of troops. The Prince suggested that an army training camp be set up on a permanent site and the place selected was Aldershot with its surrounding heath and common-land. In due course, the camp was fully equipped, including the Royal Pavilion there – the site and design of which had been chosen by the Prince – and a library of which he bore the cost. He made several visits, and it was formally opened by the Queen in July 1855. The following April they both stayed for the first time at this Royal Pavilion, followed by many more visits to Aldershot which became a source of great interest and pride to Albert.

The Great Exhibition of 1851, the first ever to be held in Britain, was the brainchild of Queen Victoria's Prince Consort and would never have taken place without his unrelenting hard work. It is the best monument to his belief in industrial Britain and to his hope that man might use his new techniques to create a better world. It was more than just a huge shop-window for British goods, a mere glorification of the new Machine Age. It was an attempt on his part to show how utility and an attractive appearance could be fused tighter. Sadly, Parliament contemptuously turned down the project leaving him with the enormous task of getting enough backers to finance it. But Albert's faith was justified. Six million people visited the Exhibition – a staggering number even allowing for foreign visitors out of the eighteen million inhabitants of England and Wales. In all there were 13,000 exhibitors accommodated in a mile of galleries covering a million square feet of floor space. Far from being a failure, as the politicians predicted, it made a profit of a quarter of a million pounds. Proudly, Victoria wrote in her *Journal* of "the patience, firmness and energy" he had displayed in organising the Exhibition in Hyde Park and added: "Albert's dearest name is immortalised with this great conception, his *own*, and my own dear country showed she was worthy of it." She opened it in May and described the occasion as "the happiest day of my life".

In the Albert Memorial, the Prince Consort's statue depicts him sitting with the catalogue of the Great Exhibition on his knees. He sits under a canopy looking south at the Albert Hall built on land bought from the profits of his Great Exhibition and he also gazes further south at the fine cluster of museums begun at his wish from those profits.

During the Crimean conflict (1854-56) Prince Albert in a memorandum pointed out how ill-prepared after forty years of peace was the British Army for engaging in such a conflict and should never have done so.

Queen Victoria in her *Journal* regrets that it had not been possible for her herself to nurse the sick and the wounded. Instead, she sent Florence Nightingale provisions, medical supplies and books, and also made money available for purchasing fresh provisions locally. She gave her secretary, Colonel Phipps, instructions to attend immediately to any of Miss Nightingale's suggestions for improving the soldiers' care.

The Queen wrote to Lord Raglan, Commander of the Army in the Crimea: "The sad privations of the army and the constant sickness are causes of the deepest concern and anxiety to me." She wanted him to be "*very* strict in seeing that no unnecessary privations are incurred by any negligence of those whose duty it is to watch over their wants". When it was decided to strike a special medal for service in the Crimea, she told the Secretary of War that she would like to present it personally with no distinction to be made between officers and privates. She wrote with enthusiasm in her *Journal*: "The rough hand of the brave and honest private soldier came for the first time in contact with that of his sovereign and Queen." What today might seem an ordinary enough event was in 1855 a breaking of social barriers that was unique.

Following her first visit accompanied by Prince Albert to the military hospital at Chatham, Queen Victoria wrote on 4th March 1855 of her desire "to pay constant visits to those noble, brave, patient men". Later, when what she had written to Florence Nightingale was published in *The Times* and elsewhere, the Queen far from being embarrassed hoped that "this might be the means of my *real* sentiments getting known by the Army". Later, she reveals that her letter had been received with the greatest enthusiasm by the men "some saying they will learn it by heart".

In a *Memorandum* dated May 1856, preserved among her papers, Queen Victoria wrote: "It is a strange omission in our Constitution that while the wife of a King has the highest rank and dignity in the realm after her husband assigned to her by the law, the husband of a Queen regnant is entirely ignored by the law. This is the most extraordinary, as a husband has in this country such particular rights and such great power over his wife, and as the Queen is married just as any other woman is, and swears to obey her lord and master, as such, while by law he has no rank or defined position. This is a strange anomaly.

"When I first married, we had difficulty on this subject; several members of the Royal Family showed bad grace in giving precedence to the Prince... Naturally, my own feeling would be to give him the same title and rank as I have, but a Titular King is a complete novelty in this country, and might be of more inconveniences than advantages to the individual who bears it. Therefore, upon mature reflexion, and after considering the question for nearly sixteen years, I have come to the conclusion that the title which is now by universal consent given him of 'Prince Consort' with the highest rank of Parliament immediately after the Queen and before every other Prince of the Royal Family, should be the one assigned to the husband of the Queen regnant, once and for all. This ought to be done before our children grow up, and it seems peculiarly easy to do so now that none of the old branches of the Royal Family are still alive."

In the past, it was these old branches who had objected. Victoria goes on: "The question has often been discussed by me with different Prime Ministers and Lord Chancellors, who have invariably agreed with me, but the wish to wait for a good moment to bring the matter before Parliament has caused one year after another to elapse without anything being done. I become now more anxious to have it settled, before our children are grown up, so that it might not appear to be done in order to guard their father's position against them personally, which could not fail to produce a painful impression upon their minds."

On 16th June, the Queen wrote to Palmerston saying that she now wished the subject to be brought before the Cabinet and asking him to read this *Memorandum* to his colleagues. She hoped, however, that he would give them strict injunctions of secrecy – "as it is of the greatest importance that the subject should be properly brought before the public and not ooze out, so that misapprehensions might arise about it in the public mind or be created by the press – before it is explained. As Lord Palmerston has not given his opinion on the subject to the Queen, she concludes that he shares her views, but it would be satisfactory for her to hear this from him."

On 15th March the following year, the Queen acknowledged receipt of the minute of the Cabinet upon *The Prince Consort Bill* and went on: "Lord Palmerston will be astonished when she tells him that the perusal of this document has caused her much surprise, so totally at variance is it with what had been expressed to her up to this moment as the opinion of Cabinet on this question."

The Queen now heard from Palmerston that the Lord Chancellor had just discovered legal reasons why the Prince could not be created Prince Consort by Act of Parliament, so the Queen retaliated by conferring the title upon him by Letters Patent on 25th June 1857.

On 12th February 1861, Victoria wrote to King Leopold that she had just celebrated the 21st anniversary of her marriage. Very few could say with her that their husbands at the end of so many years had brought to the world at large "such incalculable blessings".

Soon after this, Albert's health started to deteriorate and on 14th December he died. Victoria lived on as a widow for 40 years. On 12th May 1862 she wrote to King Leopold: "I made the effort to go and visit the truly magnificent Military Hospital at Netley in which my Angel took such immense interest and constantly went to see; I felt it a duty."

What interest the widowed Queen had in the governing of the country was influenced by what she thought Albert would have advised her. On 13th March 1865 she wrote to the Prime Minister, Palmerston, that it appeared a promise was made to Sir Alexander, the Lord Chief Justice, that she would sanction his being given a peerage, but she still retained her opinion of the absolute duty, which devolved upon her, of requiring "that peerages shall not be conferred upon any persons who do not in addition to other qualifications possess a good moral character". This she knew Sir Alexander Cockburn lacked. As a result of her disapproval, the Lord Chief Justice never received a peerage.

On 18th December Victoria wrote to the Crown Princess of Prussia: "I wished to answer what you said about the bar between high and low. What you say about it is most true (that the 'lower

classes' must rise to the upper – and not vice-versa – or the consequences are dreadful, as the first French Revolution has proved).
But, alas, that is the great danger in England now, and one which
alarms all right-minded and thinking people. The higher classes –
especially the aristocracy (with, of course, exceptions and
honourable ones) – are so frivolous, pleasure-seeking, heartless,
selfish, immoral, and gamblers, that it makes one think (just as the
Dean of Windsor said to me the other evening) of their ways
before the French Revolution. The young men are so ignorant,
luxurious and self-indulgent – and the young women so fast,
frivolous and imprudent that the danger is very great, and they
ought to be warned. The lower classes are becoming so well-
informed, are so intelligent and earn their bread and riches so
deservedly – that they cannot and ought not to be kept back – to
be abused by the wretched, ignorant, high-born beings who live
only to kill time. They must be warned and frightened or some
dreadful crash will take place."

Queen Victoria did not approve of smoking. On 6th October
1868 she wrote to Lord Charles Fitzroy, who was acting as Master
of the Household at Balmoral, to see that the smoking-room there
was always closed at twelve promptly. This was necessary for the
sake of the servants who she had heard felt these late hours very
much, as it deprived them of their well-earned sleep.

Three days later, the Queen wrote to Disraeli, the Prime Minister, that she had been greatly shocked to hear of the death of
Dr Longley, the "worthy and amiable Archbishop of Canterbury". The position of the Primate was one of such importance
and he was brought into so much personal contact with her that
she was writing to say that she thought there was no-one fitter to
succeed Longley than Dr Tait, the Bishop of London, who was
"an excellent, pious, liberal-minded, courageous man, who would
be an immense support and strength to the Church in these times
– and whose health which is not good, would be benefited by the

change". She hoped to hear from Mr Disraeli without delay on this subject. But he did not agree and recommended instead the Bishop of Gloucester and Bristol.

On 31st October the Queen replied that she could not alter her opinion that the Bishop of London was the only fit person. "The Bishop of Gloucester and Bristol, though a very good man, has not the knowledge of the world, nor the reputation and general presence which is of so great importance in a position of such very high rank, constantly called upon to perform all the highest functions in connection with the Sovereign and Royal Family."

Back came a letter from Disraeli still objecting to the Bishop of London, and so the argument went on. In the end, the Queen had her way and Dr Tait was appointed. This seems to have been the only occasion when Disraeli disagreed with the Queen. At the General Election held on 17th November that year, the Conservatives were soundly defeated. The Liberals were returned with a large majority and Gladstone became Prime Minister.

In 1861 the Prince Consort was dying. Across the Atlantic the Civil War was raging. Two Southern agents were taken off a British ship, the *Trent*, by a Northern man-of-war. British feeling at this ran high so when the Foreign Office proposed to send a strongly-worded protest, war seemed likely. The last public act of the Prince was to reword the draft in such a way as to allow the North to hand over the agents without loss of dignity and thus war was avoided.

On 21st June 1887 Queen Victoria celebrated her Golden Jubilee and wrote in her *Journal*: "This very eventful day has come and is passed... all went off admirably. Fifty years ago, I had to go with a full Sovereign's escort to St James's Palace to appear at my proclamation... The morning was beautiful and bright with a fresh air. Troops began passing early with bands playing, and one heard constant cheering... The scene outside was most animated and reminded me of the opening of the Great

Exhibition, which also took place on a very fine day... At half-past eleven we left the Palace, I driving in a handsomely gilt landau drawn by six of the Creams. Just in front rode 12 Indian officers, and in front of them my 3 sons, 5 sons-in-law, 9 grandsons, grandsons-in-law, and some of the suite. All the other Royalties went in a separate procession... At the door of Westminster Abbey I was received by the clergy, with the Archbishop of Canterbury and Dean at their head, in the copes of rich velvet and gold, which had been worn at the Coronation... The crowds from the Palace gates up to the Abbey were enormous, and there was such an extraordinary outburst of enthusiasm as I had hardly ever seen in London before; all the people seemed to be in good humour. The old Chelsea Pensioners were in a stand near the Arch... I sat alone (oh! without my beloved husband, for whom this would have been such a proud day!) where I sat forty-nine years ago... The *Te Deum*, by my darling Albert, sounded beautiful."

On 23rd September 1896, Victoria wrote in her *Journal*: "Today is the day on which I have reigned longer, by a day, than any English sovereign, and the people wished to make all sorts of demonstrations, which I asked them not to do until I had completed the sixty years next June."

On 22nd June 1897, Queen Victoria celebrated her Diamond Jubilee and wrote in her *Journal*: "A never-to-be forgotten day. No one, I believe, has met with such an ovation as was given to me, passing through those six miles of streets, including Constitutional Hill. The crowds were quite indescribable and their enthusiasm truly marvellous and deeply touching.

"At a quarter-past eleven, I started from the State entrance in an open landau... Before leaving I touched an electric button by which I started a message which was telegraphed throughout the whole Empire. It was the following: 'From my heart I thank my beloved people, May God bless them!' "

It was when on 29th January 1901 that Queen Victoria died at Osborne, that her son-in-law, the Marquess of Lorne, wrote that she sank slowly "like a great three-decker ship". Other contemporaries regarded the event as the end of an era which had been identified with stability. The tiny figure lay in state dressed in white, with her lace wedding veil covering her face. She had forbidden black because she believed that she had now been reunited with her adored Albert.

In an important letter published in the *Daily Telegraph* a hundred years later, Professor Ged Martin of Edinburgh pointed out how remarkably enduring Queen Victoria's memory has proved and that her name and title now cover almost two per cent of the world's land surface.

"She can be found in the Arctic and the Antarctic, in two Australian states (one of them, Queensland, which she named herself) and an Antipodean desert, not to mention Africa's greatest waterfall and largest lake. Victoria is commemorated in the capital of the Seychelles, a host of smaller settlements from Quebec to Hong Kong, and in three British railway stations (one of them at Southend, where her subjects at least were amused).

"Her most lavish monument stands in Calcutta, while South Australia's Lake Alexandrina provides the sole surviving clue to the Queen's original forename, dropped on her accession in 1837. Remarkably, this unintellectual woman is remembered through universities in Belfast, British Columbia, Manchester, Melbourne, Ontario and Wellington. Her cartographic impact has notably outlasted that of her chief modern rival, Joseph Stalin.

"True, the Cove of Cork, named Queenstown in her honour in 1849, reverted to the Gaelic Cobh in 1922. Yet although her statue was buried in the grounds of the local college in 1946, it was retrieved in 1995 and now has an honoured place in Cork's fine university.

"'Whoever thought Queen Victoria could die?' exclaimed the Canadian writer Lucy Maud Montgomery on hearing the news, for the monarch seemed 'a fact as enduring and unchangeable as the everlasting hills.' On the map of the world at least, Queen Victoria is immortal."

The national monument to Queen Victoria consists not only of the monument outside Buckingham Palace but also of the whole of the Mall newly made in 1903-4 together with the Admiralty Arch thus forming the most impressive roadway in London.

King Edward VII – the 'Peacemaker'

I n 1840 Queen Victoria's first child, a daughter, was born, named after her and known as the Princess Royal. A year later, on 9th November 1841, the Queen gave birth to a fine large boy, who became heir to the throne. On 6th January 1846 the Prince Consort informed Queen Victoria's confidential advisor, Christian von Stockmar: "The exaltation of Royalty is possible only through the personal character of the Sovereign. When a person enjoys complete confidence, we desire for him more power and influence in the conduct of affairs. But confidence is of slow growth." For that reason, the Prince Consort devised for his eldest son an educational plan of unparalleled rigour which made no allowance for human weakness. It was intended to prepare the future Sovereign for survival in a harsh democratic climate; but, contrary to speculation, that climate proved to be warm and genial.

Created Prince of Wales on 4th December, the boy was christened Albert Edward in St. George's Chapel, Windsor, on 25th January 1842. Many eminent men were consulted about his education after Stockmar had warned the Queen and Prince Albert that they were too young to direct this and that it was their duty to follow the advice of more experienced persons, so the child was made the unhappy subject of an educational experiment. An attempt was made to mould him in isolation from his contemporaries into a moral and intellectual paragon. Henry Birch, who had been Captain of the school at Eton and a master there for four years, after taking four University prizes at King's College, Cambridge, was selected in April 1849 at the end of a year's anxious search to serve as principal tutor to the Prince of Wales, who was taken from his nursery at the age of seven and a half by a team of tutors headed by Birch. Storm clouds gathered early. Every week-day, including Saturday, was divided into hourly or half-hourly periods, during which Birch taught the boy – Calculating, Geography and English; and other masters, who were expert in the fields, taught Religion, German, French, Handwriting, Drawing and Music. The Prince had shorter holidays and worked under more intense pressure than any schoolboy in the land.

Three years later after he had taken Holy Orders and resigned his appointment, Birch summarised his impressions of the Prince of Wales for Prince Albert. He had at first found his pupil to be extremely disobedient, impertinent to his masters and unwilling to submit to discipline. The boy had been selfish and unable even to play at any game for longer than five minutes, or attempt anything new without losing his temper. He could not endure chaff or interference of any kind. "But I thought it better, notwithstanding his sensitiveness, to laugh at him… and to treat him as I know that other boys would have treated him at an English Public School."

Although severe punishment had to be inflicted from time to time, Birch's plan had appeared to answer well – "and for the last year I saw numerous traits of a very affectionate disposition". It had, however, been almost impossible to follow out any thoroughly regular course of study because the Prince was so different from day to day and periodically displayed "symptoms of dumb insolence during which he had declined to answer questions to which he knew the answers perfectly well; but he had always evinced a most forgiving disposition after I had had occasion to complain of him to his parents, or to punish him".

Birch gave it as his opinion that many of the Prince of Wales's peculiarities arose from want of contact with boys of his own age, and from his being continually with older persons, and finding himself the centre round which everything seemed to move.

Birch was succeeded by Frederick Gibbs in January 1851 who was really hated by the Prince of Wales. He extended his lessons immediately to include six and, at one time, seven hourly periods between eight o'clock in the morning and seven o'clock in the evening on six days a week. Gibbs was ordered to ensure that the Prince of Wales and his brother Alfred were tired out physically at the end of each day by means of riding, drill and gymnastics.

After being confirmed on his sixteenth birthday the Prince was sent to live with Gibbs and a Chaplain, the Rev. Charles Tarver, at White Lodge in Richmond Park. Prince Albert gave instructions that his son should be kept away from the world for some months. The objects were to enable him to prepare for a military examination.

The Prince Consort appointed "three very distinguished young men who are to occupy in monthly rotation, a kind of equerries' place about him". Two of these had won Victoria Crosses in the Crimea, and a third in Prince Albert's words was "a thoroughly good, moral and accomplished man who never was at a public school but passed his youth in attendance on his invalid father".

In a confidential memorandum, the Prince Consort asked the three paragons to make his son the first gentleman in the country in respect of outward deportment and manners.

Both parents were impatient to form the character of the Prince of Wales before he came of age and therefore independent. "I feel very sad about him," the Queen wrote on 31st March 1858, to a relation. "He is so idle and weak. God grant that he may take things more to heart and be more serious in the future and get more power. The heart is good, warm and affectionate."

The characters of the Queen and Prince Albert had developed early as a result of the continuous stresses of life; but their son was deprived of this through confinement in a hot-house atmosphere with older men. The Prince was desperately bored at White Lodge where he dwelt in such monastic seclusion, so he was thankful when Gibbs in November 1858 resigned his post as tutor and was replaced by Colonel Robert Bruce, a kindly dapper Grenadier Guardsman who had served as Military Secretary to the Governor-General of Canada.

The Prince was exhorted to free himself from abject dependence on servants. Life was composed of duties, and in the punctual and cheerful performance of them the true soldier and gentleman must spend his time.

On 22nd November 1858 the Prince of Wales, who had been created a Knight of the Garter, was allowed to visit Berlin where his sister was awaiting the birth of her first child, the future Kaiser. The Prince Consort warned his daughter: "You will find Bertie grown up and improved. Do not miss any opportunity of urging him to hard work. Our united efforts must be directed to this end. Unfortunately, he takes no interest in anything but clothes. Even when out shooting he is more occupied with his trousers than with the game! I am particularly anxious that he should have mental occupation in Berlin. Perhaps you would let him share in some of yours, lectures, etc…"

The Prince of Wales was not formed to be an intellectual and his interest in clothes was merely an immature attempt at self-assertion. He had developed an insinuating charm which produced a gratifying effect, and his visit to Berlin, which was normally a dull place at that time of year, was a brilliant success. Many balls were given specially for him and he danced with extraordinary grace.

On 17th October 1860 the Prince went into residence at Frewin Hall, Christchuch, Oxford where selected Professors delivered special courses of lectures to him and to six other undergraduates who were hand picked to be his companions.

At the end of each of the four terms the Prince spent at Christchurch he underwent a specially conducted examination and did not do badly. The Dean was quite satisfied.

During the Long Vacation, the Prince of Wales was sent to tour Canada where he opened a railway bridge over the St. Lawrence River at Montreal and laid the foundation stone of the Federal Parliament Building at Ottawa. The whole tour was an enormous success and every city attempted to surpass the welcome which others had accorded him. On 20th September he performed his last engagement on Canadian soil and crossed the river to Detroit where he was welcomed by some thirty thousand Americans. The menace of Civil War was already evident and the Prince travelled under the name of Lord Renfrew and as a student, but that fiction was disregarded by the public. He stayed usually at hotels, and he noticed that he was expected to shake many more hands than he had in Canada.

The United States Government placed special trains at the Prince's disposal. He had an excellent reception in Chicago. He liked always to gain factual information and was interested to learn that the price of land in Dwight had risen in the past five years from 90 cents to 100 dollars an acre.

The Prince reached Washington on 3rd October and was taken to the White House in the President's carriage. James Buchanan, a venerable and handsome old gentleman who had met the Prince as a child at Buckingham Palace, welcomed his guest in a fatherly way. That evening at dinner the Prince met all the American Cabinet and their wives. He was taken next morning by the President to a reception followed by a luncheon at the Capitol.

On 5th October the President took the Prince up the Potomac to visit George Washington's house and simple grave at Mount Vernon next to which the youth planted a chestnut sapling. That symbolic act by George III's great-grandson at America's national shrine made a profound impression.

The Prince reached New York on 11th October, and General Bruce who accompanied him throughout the tour and was normally restricted to understatement wrote to Sir Charles Phipps, Keeper of the Prince's Privy Purse:

"The reception at New York has thrown all its predecessors into the shade. I despair at its ever being understood in England. Believe me, however, exaggeration is impossible. This is the culmination point of our expedition and... the affair has been one continual triumph. No doubt the primary cause has been the veneration in which Queen Victoria is held, but it is also true that finding that sentiment in operation, the Prince of Wales has so comported himself as to turn it to the fullest account and to gain for himself no small share of interest and attraction. He has undergone no slight trial, and his patience, temper and good breeding have been severely taxed. There is no doubt that he has created everywhere a favourable impression."

The Prince was driven down Broadway beside the Mayor, amid tremendous cheering, in a barouche, specially built for the occasion. As he bowed his acknowledgements, from a balcony of his Fifth Avenue hotel suite, the Prince told the Mayor that his rooms were far more comfortable than the ones he had at Buckingham Palace and Windsor Castle.

The great social event of that visit to New York was a ball at the Academy of Music for which some three thousand tickets had been issued. Dancing began at 12.30am and the Prince was vexed to find that he was expected almost all the time to partner elderly matrons instead of pretty young girls of his own age.

On 15th October the Commander-in-Chief, one of the best loved men in America, took the Prince to West Point where the cadets were paraded for his inspection. After much more crowded sightseeing, the Prince returned to England. The voyage lasted twenty-six days owing to gales and mountainous seas, and relief was felt in England when the Prince reached Plymouth at last on

15th November 1860. At Windsor he was congratulated by his parents and Queen Victoria noted that he had become extremely talkative. Everyone agreed that the tour had been immensely beneficial to him. He had discovered his métier.

After leaving Christchurch, Oxford, the Prince of Wales entered Trinity College, Cambridge, where he made more friends than he had been able to do at Oxford. His heart was now set on a period of army attachment with the Guards and on 13th March 1861 the Prince Consort agreed that his son should be subjected to a ten weeks long course of infantry training under the strictest discipline which could be devised at the Curragh Camp near Dublin during the summer vacation. Attached to the 1st Battalion Grenadier Guards, he must learn the duties of every grade from ensign upwards without being detained longer at any one than would be necessary for his thoroughly mastering it. In that way he should contrive to earn promotion every fortnight and with some exertion arrive in the ten weeks before him at the Command of a Battalion, and be made competent to manoeuvre a Brigade in the Field.

When the Prince's grandmother, the Duchess of Kent, died on 16th March Queen Victoria rebuked him for not mourning her passing with more display. He had acted in a selfish and heartless manner she told him. He diplomatically replied that stunned by the sudden blow he had not wanted to intrude while his sisters were sympathising with her so warmly and affectionately, not because he had not the same feelings as they had, but because he thought he would be in the way and that they would be a greater support to her. He added that he had ordered "some more letter paper with rather deeper black edges, as you wished".

An early marriage was regarded by Victoria and her husband as essential for the improvement of the Prince of Wales's character and he himself insisted that he would marry only for love. The Prince Consort was worried when he commenced to list personable Protestant Princesses how few there were of them who were at all attractive. The only truly beautiful one was Princess Alexandra of Denmark. The trouble was the acrimonious dispute between Germany and Denmark over Schleswig-Holstein. A secret meeting between he and the Prince of Wales was arranged in September 1861 when, under cover of continuing his military studies, he attended the autumn manoeuvres of the Prussian army near Coblenz. On 30th September the Prince went to Balmoral, where he told Queen Victoria what he thought of Alexandra, and she wrote to her daughter next day: "Bertie is decidedly pleased with her, but as for being in love, I don't think he can be, or that he is capable of enthusiasm about anything in the world."

The reason for Bertie's procrastination was because he had been having an affair with an actress in Ireland. On 16th November, the Prince Consort wrote to his eldest son "with a heavy heart upon a subject which has caused me the greatest pain I have yet felt in this life". After searching inquiry, he had learnt about it. Did this explain why Bertie was reluctant to marry? The Prince replied that he had yielded to temptation, but that the affair was now ended.

The Prince Consort forgave his son and stressed the necessity for an early marriage. "You *must* not, you *dare* not be lost. The consequences for this country, and for the world, would be too dreadful."

On the 29th of that month, the Prince Consort wrote to his eldest daughter, the Crown Princess of Germany: "I am at a very low ebb. Much worry (about which I beg you not to ask questions) have robbed me of sleep during the past fortnight. In this shattered state, I had a very heavy catarrh." There were symptoms of typhoid, and after collapsing on 2nd December, Prince Albert died on 14th December 1861.

For some months, Queen Victoria was too distressed to do anything about Bertie's marriage. His very presence in the country irked his mother. It was decided that he should be sent upon a journey to Palestine and the near East to last for many months, which his father had planned as the most important part of the youth's formal education. He left England incognito on 6th February 1862 accompanied by three equerries and a doctor, as well as by General Bruce, whose instructions were to foster above all else the plan for him to marry Princess Alexandra.

On 14th June the Prince returned from his travels and later that day Queen Victoria wrote in her *Journal*: "Bertie arrived at ½ past 5, looking extremely well... Dear Bertie was most affectionate and the tears came into his eyes when he saw me." On the days that followed, he assured her that he wanted to do everything she wished and, in particular, to meet and propose marriage to Princess Alexandra at the earliest possible moment.

Travelling as Countess of Balmoral, some weeks later, Queen Victoria stayed with her Uncle Leopold, King of the Belgians, at his Palace of Laeken outside Brussels on her way to visit the scenes of her dead husband's childhood at Coburg. Prince and Princess Christian of Denmark, with their daughters, Alix and Dagmar (later the Empress Marie Feodorovna, wife of the Tsar Alexander III of Russia) had already reached Laeken from Ostend where they had been staying. Queen Victoria wrote in her *Journal* on 3rd September: "Alexandra is lovely, such a beautiful refined profile, and quiet ladylike manner, which made a most favourable impression."

In a private talk with Prince and Princess Christian, the Queen said she hoped that their daughter would accept her son. They assured her that Bertie might hope she would do so. On 10th September, the Prince of Wales wrote his mother a letter from a hotel in Brussels, beginning: "The all-important event has taken place. I proposed to the Princess at Laeken and she accepted me; and I cannot tell you how grateful I am for it." This was followed next day by another letter to the Queen about Alexandra in which he declared: "I did not think it possible to love a person as I do her. She is so kind and good, and I feel sure will make my life a happy one. I only trust that God will give me strength to do the same for her."

At the beginning of November, Queen Victoria asked Prince Christian to bring his daughter to England and then depart immediately leaving her at Osborne and Windsor for some four to five weeks. This he did. The Queen also asked the Prince of Wales to remain abroad while Princess Alexandra was in England, and placed a royal yacht at his disposal for a Mediterranean cruise. He felt constrained to agree, although separation from his betrothed meant spending his 21st birthday abroad.

During her visit to Osborne and Windsor, Princess Alexandra completely captivated Queen Victoria, who wrote in her *Journal*: "I can't say how I and we all love her! She is so good, so simple, unaffected, frank, and cheerful, yet so quiet and gentle that her companionship soothes me. How lovely!... This jewel! She is one of those sweet creatures who seem to come from the skies to help and bless poor mortals and lighten for a time their path."

The wedding was fixed for 10th March 1863; and the Prince of Wales discovered that he had inherited an annual personal income of about £50,000 from the Duchy of Cornwall, which had been nursed most efficiently by his father, as well as a capital sum of about £600,000. £220,000 had been used a few months earlier to buy a 7,000 acre property at Sandringham.

Before his marriage, the Prince of Wales contributed £10,000 towards the building of the Mausoleum at Frogmore, and spent another £100,000 on furniture, carriages and jewellery, while the Government spent £60,000 on the drastic modernisation of Marlborough House which became his London home. He was left with an invested capital of about £270,000 which served, with the Sandringham rent-roll of between £5,000 and £7,000, to raise his annual income to a little less than £65,000.

Radicals argued that that sum ought to suffice; but extensive improvements were known to be necessary at Sandringham, and the Chancellor of the Exchequer, W.E. Gladstone, insisted that the Prince's total income ought not to amount to less than £100,000. Sir Charles Phipps, Keeper of the Privy Purse, warned Gladstone that "even with that the Prince will be unable to do much that will be expected from him". Lord Palmerston considered that the Prince was being treated shabbily. But Parliament was asked to vote only an additional £50,000, of which £10,000 was apportioned as 'pin money' to the Princess who had nothing of her own.

The Prince of Wales was warned by *The Times* that he would be expected to outshine every subject. The Prince was required, therefore, to provide the capital city of the richest and most powerful Empire on earth with a substitute Court on an income which, even when viewed against a background of Victorian money values, must appear inadequate.

In these circumstances, it is remarkable that the Prince of Wales's annual expenditure did not, from the outset, exceed his income by more than £20,000 a year. The annual deficit was met out of his capital until that was exhausted, and the Prince was then wise enough to consult and to profit from the expert advice of such successful financiers as the Rothschilds, Maurice Hirsch and Ernest Cassel.

On 7th March 1863 Princess Alexandra, accompanied by her parents and relatives, reached England from Copenhagen and were taken by the Prince of Wales to stay at Windsor Castle. Queen Victoria greeted them on arrival, but still feeling too desolate over the death of Prince Albert did not appear at dinner, which she took in a separate room. She noted however in her Journal that immediately before the meal: "Alix knocked at the door, peeped in and came and knelt before me with that sweet loving expression that spoke volumes. I was much moved and kissed her again and again."

At the wedding service in St. George's Chapel on 10th March 1863, the bride wore a white satin gown trimmed with garlands of orange blossom and puffings of white tulle with Honiton lace. She had cried during the morning at parting from her mother, but she exclaimed with spirit to the Crown Princess of Prussia: "You may think that I like marrying Bertie for his position; but if he were a cowboy I would love him just the same and would marry no one else."

After lunching with thirty-six other Royalties (but not with the Queen) the Prince and Princess of Wales left for a week's honeymoon at Osborne.

On 7th April the married couple moved into Marlborough House. Then began such a season as London had never previously known, and Disraeli described it as a Royal public honeymoon extended over months. As ball succeeded ball amid a whirl of fêtes and receptions, processions and ceremonies, the Prince of Wales, in the flower of his lusty youth and with the most beautiful Princess in Europe at his side, inaugurated within inimitable gusto a social sovereignty which lasted until he died.

The Society which acclaimed the Prince and Princess of Wales was supported by twenty-five million inhabitants of the British Isles who were rapidly being transformed into an urban prole-tariat. Housing conditions were appalling, but an expanding economy was raising the living standards of all except the poorest, who existed almost like animals.

Detesting arrogance and despising snobbery, the Prince of Wales helped to adapt society to the changing spirit of his age.

On 24th June 1863 the Queen described her son and daughter-in-law as in the process of becoming "nothing but puppets running about for show all day and all night". A fortnight earlier the Queen had written to the Crown Princess of Prussia: "Bertie and Alix left Frogmore today both looking as ill as possible.

We are all seriously alarmed about her. For although Bertie says he is so anxious to take care of her, he goes on going out every night till she will become a skeleton. Oh, how different poor foolish Bertie is to adored Papa whose gentle, loving, wise, motherly care of me, when he was not twenty-one, exceeded everything!" Three days later Victoria wrote: "Oh, what will become of the poor country when I die! I foresee, if Bertie succeeds, nothing but misery and he would do anything he was asked and spend his life in one whirl of amusements, as he does now. It makes me very sad and anxious."

On 7th January five years later, Victoria wrote to the Prince of Wales that the 'Lower Orders' were daily becoming more well informed and more intelligent and would deservedly work themselves up to the top by their own merits, labour and good conduct. She went on: "Many, many, with whom I have conversed tell me that at no time for the last 60 to 70 years was frivolity, the love of pleasure, self-indulgence, luxury and idleness (producing ignorance) carried to such an excess as now in the Higher Classes, and it resembles the time before the French Revolution, and I must – alas – admit that this is true. It is most alarming, although you do not observe it, nor will you *hear* it; but those who do not live in the gay circle of fashion, and who view it calmly, are greatly, seriously alarmed. And in THIS lies the REAL danger of the present times! The Aristocracy and the Higher Classes must take great care; or their position may become very dangerous. I shall do what I can in this direction, but you can do more, and so can dear Alix, to whom I wish you to show this letter as I have often talked to her on these subjects."

Philip Magnus in his biography of King Edward VII comments: "This wise letter was in part the fruit of Queen Victoria's vivid recollection of the quasi-revolutionary agitation of the 1820's, 30's, and 40's, which had coloured her childhood and youth and it had been buried so deeply in her mind that she noted occasionally with disapproval that even Princess Alix was become "a little grand".

Queen Victoria was fond of saying that a Prince in the modern world could only maintain his position by his character.

The restraints to which he had been subjected to as a boy caused the Prince of Wales to dive headlong into all the varied delights which a rich and sophisticated society had to offer and he paid no attention to his mother's reiterated objections to the conduct or characters of his most intimate friends.

It became the custom of the Prince of Wales to visit the French Riviera at the beginning of March for five weeks, which included a few days in Paris at either end. He sent his yacht ahead, which he often made his headquarters, and he attended fêtes, dinners, balls and suppers almost every night before returning refreshed to Marlborough House to face the rigours of the London season.

Most of the Prince's public engagements were taken during the summer months. He accumulated a number of honorary Presidencies, Chairmanships, Governorships, and Colonelcies. For example, he became in 1863 President of the Society of Arts, Chairman of the Governors of Welling College, a Governor of the Charterhouse and of Christ's Hospital and Regimental Colonel of the 10th Hussars. On an average of twenty-seven days a year during the last 1860's, the Prince attended public dinners, laid foundation stones, opened buildings or inspected institutions; and the light in which he regarded these duties are shown in a letter which he wrote to former tutor, F.W. Gibbs, who had expressed a hope that the Prince would not decline to open the new buildings of Glasgow University, and the Prince replied: "I quite agree with you that the duty (which, after all, will be a very easy one) which I should have to perform, has for its object, a National one; and I shall never shrink from coming forward (however inconvenient to myself) when asked for such an occasion. "But I am asked, if once, at least thirty times in the course of the year to do things which only make me an advertisement, and a puff to the object in view; and I think you will agree with me that I ought to think twice before (using a slang expression) being 'let in' to such things."

The public sector of the nation's economy was extremely narrow at that time, but the Prince duly opened the new buildings at Glasgow as requested. He had become an accomplished and fluent public speaker and he never used notes on such occasions after passing a difficult test on 18th June 1865. He was called upon unexpectedly to propose or respond to five toasts that evening at a dinner in aid of the Duke of Cambridge's Homes for Soldiers' Wives, and his diary recorded: "All went off very well but it was a great ordeal for me to go through."

Queen Victoria approved of the Prince and Princess of Wales driving out in Hyde Park and wrote in her *Journal*: "We live in radical times and the more the People see Royalty the better it is for the People and the Country."

Sir Bartle Freer wrote to Lord Carrington that the idolatry now lavished upon the Prince of Wales by the great mass of the British people was not diminished by the few human faults which he was much too straightforward to attempt to conceal. The Prince Consort, despite his outstanding qualities and virtues, had never inspired a tithe of the loyalty and affection which his son commanded without effort, because he was regarded as the typical Englishman living the kind of princely life which the majority of his fellow countrymen wished him to live in that age and which, in his position, they would have lived and enjoyed themselves.

Contemporary critics often compiled summaries of the way in which Edward VII apportioned his time. According to his diary as the Prince of Wales, 1897 was a typical year during which he performed twenty major public engagements. July was the busiest month. On the 5th, he conducted the Queen around the Agricultural Exhibition, three days later he laid the foundation of the new wing of the Royal Hospital for Incurables at West Hill,

Putney Heath. On the 9th, he visited the Academy of Music for the Blind when Princess Alexandra presented prizes, which she did again on the 15th when they both went to the National Orphan Home at Ham. Two days later, he laid another foundation stone at the new wing of the Hospital for Consumption at Brompton; and lastly he presented prizes on the 26th at the Royal Hospital School, Greenwich.

The Prince also visited many artists' studios, attended committee meetings, and after seven of the eighty occasions on which he went to the theatre, opera or ordinary concerts, the proceeds were devoted to charities. He attended the House of Lords nineteen times during 1879.

Sir Frederick Ponsonby, Edward VII's private secretary, wrote in his memoirs that the King on his State Visits abroad, after his accession to the throne in 1901, made all the arrangements and supervised all the details himself. Ponsonby was surprised to find that some of the most significant aspects of tours were being arranged personally by the King while it was in progress. Two years later, he notified President Emile Loubet of France that he had ordered four battleships of the British Fleet to leave Gibraltar on 12th April in time to salute the President on his arrival in Algiers.

Touched by that unexpected courtesy at a time when Anglo-French relations were otherwise strained, Loubet telegraphed warm thanks and formally invited the King to visit France on the way home from the Mediterranean. The Foreign Secretary, Lord Lansdowne, warned him that such a visit might be dangerous, but Edward accepted at once and ordered his Ambassador in Paris to prepare a detailed programme forthwith. The King first went to Rome where despite angry protests from fanatical Protestants, he called on the Pope, then travelled north to Paris where he was to enjoy the finest hours of his reign. On arrival he was welcomed by Loubet who drove at his side at the head of a procession along the *Champs Elysées* to the British Embassy. The reaction from the crowd was respectful but cool. As always, Edward himself appeared to exude warmth and friendliness, and wrote Philip Magnus, his biographer, every gesture which he made was stamped "with a calculated and inimitable geniality developed to the pitch of a fine art".

That evening, after dining at the British Embassy, the King and the President attended the play at the *Théâtre Français* where the King's reception was indifferent to the point of iciness, but during the first interval he noticed the great actress, Mlle. Jeanne Granier, standing in the foyer at the centre of a group of friends. Without hesitation, King Edward walked over to her, kissed her hand and exclaimed: "Mademoiselle, I remember applauding you in London where you represented all the grace and spirit of France." The ice seemed to dissolve almost visibly, as that compliment was repeated everywhere and Paris buzzed with it within twenty-four hours.

On the morning of 2nd May, King Edward drove with the President to a review held in his honour at Vincennes and it was easy to perceive a marked increase in cordiality among the onlookers, and a large crowd cheered warmly for the first time when he reached the *Hôtel de Ville* at 11.45. In a short extempore speech, the King assured his hosts that he would never forget their beautiful city to which he had returned with the greatest pleasure and where he had always felt at home.

The climax was reached that evening, when the King drove to a gala performance at the *Opéra* after dining with the President at the *Elysée*. King Edward's carriage had difficulty in making its way through the milling crowds which seemed to have gone mad and cheered continuously in French variations of "Good old Teddy!" From then on, the King was greeted everywhere with thunderous popular applause and well-meant shouts of *"Vive Édouard!"* and *"Notre bon Édouard!"* and it became evident, as

Sir Edmund Monson, the British Ambassador in Paris, wrote to
Lord Lansdowne: "The visit has been a success here more
complete than the most sanguine optimist could have foreseen.
The personality of the King and the indefatigable readiness with
which he adapted himself to the overcharged programme of
functions... the reappearance of the frequent visitor of former
years, the well-known and popular Prince of Wales, coming back
to his old friends as King of England, returning to the capital for
which he had never concealed his predilection, aroused a feeling
of gratification only equalled by the satisfaction of that large body
of politicians who, from motives of reason, reflection and clear
comprehension of this country's interests, have always systemat-
ically favoured the *'Entente Cordiale'*."

Throughout King Edward's five weeks' tour that summer he
would usually discuss the day's programme over breakfast with
Charles Hardinge, an under-secretary in the Foreign Office, who
wrote in his memoirs: "Often I had to suggest a visit which I knew
would be irksome, or that he should see somebody that I knew he
did not want to see and he would exclaim, 'No, no, damned if I
will do it!' But he always did it, how ever tiresome it might be to
him, without my having to argue the point or in fact say another
word. He had a very strong sense of the duties which his position
entailed and he never shirked them. On Sunday, 3rd May, for
example, after attending church and receiving several friends, he
was tired and ravenous for luncheon, which he was to take with
the French Foreign Minister, but he consented to present a medal
first to an old soldier who had served in the Crimea."

In addition to the five grades of the Royal Victorian Order,
King Edward always distributed on his tours abroad many
jewelled tie pins, cuff links, cigarette cases, in gold or silver
bearing his royal cipher picked out in diamonds or enamel. On
this notable visit to Paris he took great pleasure in distributing
these presents on a lavish scale.

In June 1907, on a visit to London, the King of Siam hoped to receive the Order of the Garter, but King Edward refused to confer it upon the ruler of a country then of minor importance. Some Siamese ministers were terrified that they might be decapitated for having misled their Sovereign. The British Foreign Office, which had not been guiltless, was most anxious to avoid unpleasantness and left it to Grey, the Foreign Secretary himself, to press the matter upon King Edward who would have nothing to do with it and won an additional victory in a dispute with the Treasury about the broad principle of meeting expenses of foreign royal visits. It had been agreed at the start of the reign, that the State should defray any incurred by King Edward in entertaining foreign rulers, but the Treasury had expected that a distinction would be made between visits of political value and those which were private.

King Edward regarded all visits by foreign sovereigns as State occasions and he refused to compromise in any way. He would not stand such an evasion by the Treasury of what had been agreed in 1901. So that attempt at cheese-paring was abandoned and to recuperate from the stress caused, King Edward went for a cure at the spa of Marienbad. While there, he attended at the theatre on 29th August, a play called *Die Holle* (The Underworld) advertised as a melodrama. It was in poor taste and the King was bored so left after the start of the second act, which was reported in English newspapers and to his astonishment he received piles of letters expressing loyal approval for the stand that he was alleged to have taken in the cause of morality. The Bishop of Ripon sent a fulsome letter on behalf of the Church of England, and the King's secretary asked what reply should be sent. Edward exclaimed: "Tell the truth, of course. I have no wish to pose as a protector of morals, especially abroad."

On 31st August 1909, King Edward was informed by telegram that the Anglo-Russian Convention had been signed that day in

St. Petersburg by Sir Arthur Nicolson, the British Ambassador, and by Alexander Isvolsky, the Russian Foreign Minister. That agreement, to which King Edward and the Emperor Nicholas added their signatures three weeks later, had been under discussion for four years, and it was the triumph of King Edward's policy of which the Anglo-French *entente* was the first step. During the course of these difficult negotiations, he had protested many times that, although Persia was divided into spheres of influence between the high contracting Powers, the predominantly British interest in the Persian Gulf was neglected. Isvolsky feared a clash with Germany in that area on the issue of the projected Berlin-Baghdad railroad, but Sir Charles Hardinge, the King's close adviser, assured him that the mere existence of a treaty was of greater importance than its actual content. He wrote in his private papers: "Although its terms might have been more advantageous to England in certain respects, it served its purpose and maintained peace and friendly relations between England and Russia for ten years."

King Edward was delighted. He had already telegraphed some days earlier inviting Isvolsky to come to Marienbad. He informed Hardinge that Isvolsky had accepted, and Hardinge replied on 1st September: "That interview will complete the chain of interviews of last month, which I feel confident will be productive of good results." He added that King Edward would be well-advised to lavish flattery upon the Minister, who was "essentially a vain man".

Four days later, the King entertained Isvolsky to lunch and after lauding him for his service to the cause of peace, told him that all future difficulties would be easily solved in a spirit of give-and-take, now that the ice was broken. On 6th September Edward returned rejoicing to Buckingham Palace.

Edward VII was called the Peacemaker. In 1895, when he was still Prince of Wales, Venezuela claimed a large part of British

Guiana. The US President Cleveland bellicosely threatened to use force in favour of Venezuela. War might have broken out but for the Prince. Joseph Pulitzer, proprietor of the *New York World*, cabled an invitation to him to state his views. Edward composed a perfect reply which he showed to Lord Salisbury who reminded him that it was his constitutional duty to be silent, but the Prince felt so strongly about the wicked absurdity of an Anglo-American war that he rejected that advice and cabled on 23rd December 1895 to Pulitzer: "I thank you for telegram. I earnestly trust and cannot but believe present crisis will be arranged in a manner satisfactory to both countries and will be succeeded by the same warm feeling of friendship which has existed between them for so many years."

Published on Christmas Eve, such a helpful and conciliatory gesture swung American opinion in favour of Britain, and Cleveland, who was standing for re-election as President, thought it wise to cease threatening war. So the dispute was submitted to arbitration which resulted in a favourable award to Britain.

When on 7th June 1905 the Norwegians dissolved their country's union with Sweden which had existed since 1815 under the Swedish Crown, the official British attitude was one of strict neutrality, but King Edward knew his bellicose cousin the German Kaiser planned to install one of his younger sons on the Norwegian throne. This Edward felt would upset the balance of power in Europe so he persuaded his son-in-law, Prince Charles of Denmark, to stand for election and was immensely relieved when Charles was elected by a majority of 5 to 1 in a referendum. As King Haakon VII, Charles proved an admirable King and relations between Norway and Britain were greatly strengthened as a result.

George V – the 'Sailor King' and Queen Mary – 'Grandma England'

I t is a minute before midnight on May 26th 1867 and in the room at Kensington Palace which 40 years earlier had been the nursery of Queen Victoria, Princess Mary Adelaide of Teck has brought into the world an infant princess who is to be christened Victoria Mary Augusta Louisa Olga Pauline Claudine Agnes – and who for the first 25 years of her life is to be known to the public as Princess May – and whom her grand-daughter, Elizabeth II, was to call "Grandma England". Her father was the Duke of Teck, the only child of the marriage of Duke Alexander of Wurtemburg to Claudine Countess Rhédey. It was from this Hungarian beauty that the future Queen Mary was to inherit many traits in her character and appearance – her eyebrows, her eyes, set at an angle, the manner in which she smoked cigarettes, her love of jewels, and the way she wore them. The Duke of Teck had been brought up in Vienna where he acquired the cultured outlook of the old Habsburg monarchy, and much of this he transmitted to his daughter. His wife, Princess May's mother, was the child of the Duke of Cambridge, the youngest son of George III. The new baby was therefore a cousin of Queen Victoria who came to see it in June and who described it as "a very fine child with quantities of hair brushed into a curl on the top of its head".

The Duchess of Teck was well loved by the people of London. She was very fond of entertaining. Her hospitality was lavish and debts began to accumulate. So oblivious was she of her actual financial position that on one occasion, when opening a new church hall at Kensington, to the building of which one of the Tecks' chief creditors, Mr. John Barker, the Kensington grocer had largely contributed, the Duchess greatly astonished the assembled company by turning gracefully towards him on the platform and announcing with a bewitching smile: "And now I must propose a special vote of thanks to Mr. Barker, to whom we all owe so much."

Though the Duchess loved the beautiful apartments in Kensington Palace that Queen Victoria had allotted to them, she became worried that the harmful effluvia from the Kensington ponds might give the children illnesses, so she persuaded Queen Victoria to let them have a royal residence, White Lodge, in Richmond Park. This, besides being healthier for the children, provided an occupation for the Duke of Teck who became a passionate gardener. But even out at Richmond Park, the Tecks found it impossible to live within their income. Their debts grew so large that they had to cut down expenses by going to live in Florence in 1883. The fact that her parents were always so impecunious taught Princess May never to live above her income and to sympathise with people who were not financially well off. In Florence, she spent her afternoons going to museums and finding it much more to her taste than tea and gossip with the English colony. Nevertheless, she was a high spirited girl with a lively sense of humour and when she went to stay at the Court of Wurtemburg in Stuttgart, she would sometimes hide behind a pillar at the court ball and trip up some pompous functionary as he went by, or she would suddenly cause confusion in the quadrille by pushing some stately performer in the back. But in Florence, further worries were to overtake the Tecks for, in the early Spring of 1884, the Duke of Teck had a severe paralytic stroke brought on by his financial worries. He was left a sick man, prematurely aged in his 50's. So they returned to England and Princess May and her three brothers started seeing more and more of their cousins, the children of the Prince and Princess of Wales.

1. Queen Victoria and Albert, her Prince Consort

2. Queen Victoria and Prince Albert with their children, left to right: Alfred, Edward, Alice, Helena and Victoria, painted by Franz Winterhalter, 1846

*3. State portrait of Queen Victoria
by Franz Winterhalter, 1859*

4. *Queen Victoria on holiday at Cimiez on the Cote d'Azur in France*

5. *Portrait of King Edward VII*
   by Charles Buchel, 1902

6. *Queen Mary and King George V with Queen Alexandra centre at the Royal Pavilion, 1919*

7. *George V at the helm of the yacht Britannia, 1924*

8. *Queen Mary visiting the annual workers' exhibition*
of First World War veterans, 1933

9. *Edward VIII, then Prince of Wales, calling at*
a miner's cottage in Durham, 1935

10. *Engagement photograph of King George VI, then Duke of York, and Lady Elizabeth Bowes-Lyon, 1923*

11. *King George VI and Queen Elizabeth visiting workman in a bomb damaged area of London, 1940*

*12. Queen Elizabeth II with Prince Philip
at the time of her accession, 1952*

*13. Queen Mary holding her great grandson, Prince Charles,
in the christening robes which had first been used by
Queen Victoria's children, 1949*

14. *Queen Elizabeth II, the Duke of Edinburgh, Prince Charles and Princess Anne at the state opening of Parliament, 1967*

15. *Elizabeth, the Queen Mother celebrates her 80th birthday in the company of her daughter, Queen Elizabeth II, 1980*

*16. Charles and Diana, the Prince and Princess of Wales, with
their first-born son Prince William at Kensington Palace, London*

At the age of 24, in 1891, Princess May was still unmarried and occupying herself with reading and study, helping her mother with her many charities. Just at this time, Queen Victoria was feeling increasingly worried with the way her grandson, the Prince of Wales's son, Prince Eddy, was growing up. He was wayward and self-indulgent. Queen Victoria decided the best thing for him would be marriage to a strong-minded, sensible Princess, and who better, she decided, than Princess May, so she sent for her. After arranging 1,800 garments for the London Needlework Guild at White Lodge on November 4th 1891, Princess May with her eldest brother caught the night train to Aberdeen, thence to Balmoral to stay with Aunt Queen for 10 days. Queen Victoria was highly satisfied. She wrote to the Prince of Wales: "I cannot say enough good of her. She's a particularly nice girl, so quiet, yet cheerful, and so very carefully brought up – and so sensible. She's grown very pretty." To the Duchess of Teck Queen Victoria wrote: "May is a dear charming girl with such good manners and so sensible and so unfrivolous. She was in great good looks."

On December 8th, the Prince of Wales wrote to his mother from Marlborough House: "You may I think make up your mind quite easily about Eddy and that he has made up his mind too. He is going to propose to May, but we thought it best not to rush things and as she's coming to visit us with her parents for Christmas at Sandringham, everything can be arranged satisfactorily then."

But the Prince of Wales was overlooking Eddy's own character. Once an idea was put into his head, he acted on it. He was now all bent on marrying Princess May. On the very day on which his father was writing to Queen Victoria about the importance of a decent interval, Prince Eddy was staying under the same roof as Princess May at the house of the Danish Minister to the Court of St. James. In her diary, Princess May wrote that Thursday the 8th December 1891 was a dull day. This referred to the weather only. In the evening there was a ball and while it was in progress Prince Eddy led his cousin into his hostess's boudoir, and proposed to her. In those days, royal marriages were seldom made for love. Princess May had been brought up to venerate the throne and to believe that her first duty as a Princess was to help support it. For this reason, she accepted Eddy. She also liked him, though she did not know him very well. The engagement had taken place earlier than expected and it was not possible to keep it a secret. A public announcement was made. Prince Eddy, having proposed in the impetuosity of the moment, was now blissfully happy. Princess May infected him with her own high spirits. They drove out in London incognito in the Prince of Wales's private hansom. They went to Modern Venice at Olympia and floated in a gondola around a replica of part of the Grand Canal.

January 1892 was a particular bad one in London. A thick yellow fog had descended at Christmas and lasted into the New Year. A family party at Sandringham assembled to celebrate Prince Eddy's birthday on the 8th January. On that very day he fell ill with influenza which developed into pneumonia. He became delirious and on 14th January he died. On 20th January he was buried at Windsor. The most touching moment was when the Duke of Teck handed the Prince of Wales what was to have been Princess May's bridal wreath of orange blossom which was then laid upon the coffin. Princess May returned with her parents to White Lodge. She wrote in her diary: "It is so difficult to begin one's life again after such a shock, even reading of which I am so fond is a trouble to me, I cannot settle down to anything. As for writing, I simply cannot write – it is so dreadful to have to open the wound afresh."

The death before marriage of the Heir Presumptive meant that the throne of England must ultimately descend to Eddy's only brother, Prince George, who was 26 and unmarried. He was recovering from a dangerous attack of typhoid fever which had laid him low in the Autumn of 1891. He was now convalescent, but his nerves was shattered by his brother's death and he was suffering from insomnia. But it had become vital for him to marry and have a family. Now, Alexandra, Princess of Wales, had a younger sister, Princess Dagmar, who, in 1865, had been engaged to the heir to the Russian throne, the Tsarevitch Nicholas, who had, however, died before their marriage, leaving Princess Alexandra in exactly the same position as that of Princess May 27 years later. In the year following the Tsarevitch's death, Princess Dagmar of Denmark had married his brother, Alexander, and the marriage had proved a tremendous success. Princess Dagmar was now the Empress Marie Feodorovna and the mother of six children. This successful precedent was first commented on by the Duchess of Teck as one that might again be applied in the case of Princess May. Soon, all London was buzzing with the idea. This highly delicate subject was never mentioned to Princess May, but she was affronted and embarrassed by the idea and her parents found that when in March 1892 they took her abroad to recuperate from sorrow, she refused to go back to England when they did.

Prince George had loved his brother, Eddy, with the protective love of a stronger character for a weaker one. He liked to talk to Princess May about him. For the rest of his life George always wrote his letters with Prince Eddy's pen. Their common desolation began to draw the couple together. At the end of March, George came with his father, the Prince of Wales, aboard the yacht Nérine to Cannes where the Tecks were staying. George sent Princess May a little note – "Papa and I are coming over to Cannes towards the end of the week for a few days (incog) and so I hope I shall see you then. We hope one day you will give us a little dinner. We are going to stay at a quiet hotel, only don't say anything about it. Goodbye, dear Miss May, ever your very loving cousin, Georgie." Although the visit was supposed to be incognito, it was quite impossible to keep it a secret and it created a flurry of excitement among the English residents – and the public back home. But when George returned to England, the Tecks moved on to the court of their relatives at Stuttgart. At last in July they returned to White Lodge.

In May Prince George had been created Duke of York by Queen Victoria. He was in every way the opposite to his brother. Shorter, with fair hair, bright blue eyes, very red lips, white teeth and a beard. He was high-spirited, independently-minded, candid and had a very high sense of duty. His special form of humour was chaff.

A year passed and then on 2nd May 1893 Prince George proposed to Princess May in the garden of the Sheen Home of his brother-in-law, the Duke of Fife, and his sister, Princess Louise. The final verdict on the wisdom of this match comes best from George himself. When King George V on 22nd December 1911, he wrote – "We suit each other admirably and I thank God every day that he should have brought us together, especially after the tragic circumstances of dear Eddy's death when people only said I married you out of sympathy and pity. That shows how little the world really knows what it is talking about."

Every day of their engagement found them more and more drawn towards each other. In a letter dated 3rd July he added: "It is just two months today that we were engaged. I loved you then very much. Now I adore you. I feel so happy but I don't know how to thank you enough for having made me so."

Lady Geraldine Somerset wrote in her journal on the night of 6th July 1893: "May's wedding day, the greatest success ever seen or heard of! Not a hitch from first to last, not an if or a but! Everything went absolutely right. First of all, it was the most heavenly day that could be. Piccadilly was beautifully decorated, but anything to equal the loveliness of St. James's Street I never saw. It was like a bower from end to end – garlands of green and bracelets of flowers." Princess May's wedding dress had a train of silver and white brocade woven in the looms of Spitalfields and embroidered with a design of roses, shamrocks and thistles in silver on a white background. She wore a small lace veil fastened with a diamond rose of York. For going away, she changed into a dress of creamy white poplin and a similar cape in lace – on her head she wore a small golden bonnet trimmed with white ostrich plumes and white rosebuds tied under the chin with white velvet strings. Then the couple left for York Cottage near Sandringham which was to be their home for the next 33 years.

Some months later Prince George wrote to his wife: "I know I am vain enough to think that I am capable of loving anybody (who returns my love) with all my heart and soul and I am sure that I have found that person in my sweet little May. When I asked you to marry me, I was very fond of you, but not very much in love with you, but I saw in you the person I was capable of loving more deeply, if you only returned that love. I have tried to understand you and to know you and with the happy result that I know now that I do love you, darling girl, with all my love, and I am simply devoted to you. I adore you, sweet May. I cannot say more than that."

Princess May discovered that her husband liked reading aloud so she encouraged him to read to her whatever he fancied. She wrote to her old governess after the first week of the honeymoon: "George is a dear. He likes reading to people, so I jumped at this and he is going to read me some of his favourite books. Yesterday, he read part of Greville's memoirs to me – most amusing. It makes life very pleasant doing things together in this way and I am very glad I am married and I don't feel it at all strange – in fact I feel as if I had been married for years and quite settled down. This cottage is very nice, but very small. However, I think we can make it quite charming." Then in August, the newly-weds went to Osborne on the Isle of Wight to stay with Queen Victoria, who wrote in he diary: "I cannot say how much pleased I am and we all are with dear May. She is so unaffected and sensible, and so very distinguished and dignified in her manners, and very civil to everyone. She is very pretty and the more I see her the more I like and admire her."

In London they were allotted York House in St. James's Street as their home and here on 23rd June 1894 her first child was born, later to become, of course, the Duke of Windsor. Seven years later in 1901, Queen Victoria passed away. She had grown fonder of Princess May during that time and in another letter she wrote to her: "Every time I see you I love and respect you more and more and I am so truly thankful that Georgie has a partner to help and encourage him in his difficult position."

With the accession of King Edward VII, the couple became Prince and Princess of Wales and moved to Marlborough House. Their first official duty was to go to Australia to open the first Federal Parliament of that country. It was a triumph for Princess May. Every state fell in love with her looks, her smile, her grace of manner. Lady Mary Lygon wrote: "She's at last coming out of her shell and will electrify them at home as she has everyone here." On their return, the couple took up residence at Marlborough House and its redecoration and furnishing gave her a great deal of pleasure. Princess May excelled at that sort of thing. All her life she was interested also in modern developments. The advent of motor-cars pleased her and as early as July 1903, she was writing of driving in her motor-car in Cornwall. Bicycling for women, which had come into vogue, appealed less to her. Although her husband and her sisters-in-law were all bicycling enthusiasts and on wet afternoons would bicycle round and round the ballroom of Sandringham House, Princess May confined her exercise to pedaling a large tricycle.

It is well known now that King George V's relations were not strong with his children, far from ideal in fact. Their happiest childhood memories were of the periods when they were alone with their mother. She would then display for their benefit all her gaiety, all the pent up high spirits of her youthful days at White Lodge. The Duke of Windsor in his memoirs wrote: "Although Mamma backed up my Father in all matters of discipline, she never failed to take our side whenever in her judgement he was being too harsh with us. It was Mamma's habit to rest in her boudoir before dinner. At 6.30 we were called in from the school room. She would be in negligée resting on the sofa, and when we were gathered around her on little chairs she would read and talk to us. Looking back upon this scene, I am sure that my cultural instruction began at my mother's knees. The years that she lived abroad as a young woman had mellowed her outlook, and reading and observation had equipped her with a prodigious knowledge of royal history. Her soft voice, her cultivated mind, the cosy room overflowing with personal treasures were all inseparable ingredients of the happiness I associated with this last hour of my day as a child. Being practical by nature, my mother also utilised the time to teach us how to make woollen comforters for her many charities." And whilst the children gathered round with their mother playing some educational card game, their father would be shut up in his library alone working at his stamp collection or reading *The Times*. In October 1905 the new Prince and Princess of Wales went on a state visit to India. May had read all the books she could beforehand from history to religion, so that she was able to take a keen interest in all she saw. India had a profound effect upon her. It is no exaggeration to say that she fell in love with the country and ever afterwards a certain dreamy note would enter her voice when she spoke of India. "Lovely India, beautiful India," she used to murmur like some incantation. In India, her love of the picturesque was amply satisfied and it was with regret that she left for home after four months.

In 1907 Princess May celebrated her 40th birthday. The next few years were not very exciting ones. She spent a great deal of time with her lifelong friend, Lady Maud Stephen, who shared with her a love of collecting. They would discuss sales rooms and galleries, exchange marked sales catalogues, and admire each other's newest acquisitions with the zeal of true collectors. Princess May's instincts were essentially conservative. Her aim was to preserve as much of the old world of manners and tradition as was possible before all was engulfed in oblivion by the swift developments of modern times. All she knew she herself acquired by painstaking reading and careful observation, by cross-examining museum curators, art dealers and collectors whenever these crossed her path. This passion provided her with an absorbing hobby and incidentally enriched the royal collection with many first-rate pieces of furniture or plate which had been lost through history, upheaval or neglect in the past. Princess May, and later as Queen Mary, when visiting homes of friends, acquaintances and strangers, sometimes self-invited, would stand in front of some antique she coveted and pronounce in measured tones: "I am caressing it with my eyes!" If that evoked no impulsive gesture of generosity, she would resume her tour but, on taking her leave, would pause on the doorstep and ask: "May I go back and say goodbye to that dear little cabinet?" Should even that touching appeal fail to melt the granite heart of her host, her letter of thanks might include a request to buy the piece, which few could resist. Lord Lincolnshire demanded and received £300 for his Derby biscuit group of the sons of George III. And when Lord and Lady Lee were asked to sell a little portrait of Charles II, they replied that they would be honoured if the Queen would accept it as a gift. This she accepted and sent in return an inscribed photograph framed as she explained "in Indian brocade which I bought myself at Benares".

On 6th May 1910, Edward VII died. May's Aunt Augusta, who knew her well, commented: "She will indeed be a Queen!" The new King disliked double names and had never cared for the way his wife signed letters and official papers with her first two names, Victoria Mary. He now told her that as Queen she must drop one or other of them. They both agreed she could not be called Queen Victoria, so she was styled 'Queen Mary'. She wrote to her Aunt Augusta: "It strikes me as curious to be rechristened at the age of 43."

As Queen Consort, Queen Mary now dedicated her life entirely to the service of the people and the monarchy. She sacrificed everything to her husband's needs and peace of mind. Kingship meant that she saw little of him. He would work at his despatch boxes far into the night. On 31ˢᵗ October 1910 she received a letter from George who was away at Sandringham, a letter which she treasured all the rest of her life. "This is the first letter I have written to you since our lives have been entirely changed by darling Papa having been taken from us. I fear, darling, my nature is not demonstrative, but I want you to understand that I an entirely grateful to you for all you have done and to thank you from the bottom of my heart for your love and for the enormous help and comfort which you have been to me in my new position. My love grows stronger for you every day as well as my admiration, and I thank God that he has given me such a darling devoted wife as you are."

In 1911 the Great Coronation Durbar was held in Delhi when King George V was crowned Emperor of India. He became the first British Monarch to visit the East since Richard I and the only British King Emperor to visit his Indian dominions in Imperial state. It was his own idea to go out to India and hold the Coronation Durbar in person. Those who were present bore witness that it was a ceremony of such magnificence that they have never seen anything to approach it anywhere in the world ever since. Queen Mary was once more enchanted by India and her regal bearing and manner made the trip another personal triumph for her.

Right from the beginning of the reign, the new King and Queen both began to feel that it was part of their duties to examine living conditions in the industrial regions for themselves. Consequently, they undertook a series of tours of the mining and industrial areas in 1912 and 1913. It was the first time a British monarch had ever done this. Queen Mary went to the pitheads of the various collieries, riding in the colliery trams and chatting with the men and boys as they emerged grimy from beneath ground. For the first time, a Queen visited miners' wives in their cottages and accepted cups of tea from them. A Labour politician once remarked that Queen Mary would have made an excellent factory inspector. The Queen had indeed a grasp of essentials. She could not for instance be dazzled by the bright scheme of decoration of a new ward in a maternity hospital, but would quickly perceive and point out that unshaded lights were bad for the babies' eyes.

The new King and Queen felt more at ease with British working people than they did with the members of London society. Whatever fashionable people in the capital might say about the dull tone of the new Court, the country at large were slowly becoming aware of the Queen Consort's particular qualities and aims.

In May 1913, Queen May and King George went to the wedding of the Kaiser's only daughter. Queen Mary scored yet another personal triumph. She dazzled everybody with her magnificent dresses and diamonds and her royal approach. Queen Mary could, when she wished it, adorn herself with royal splendour. She regarded these trappings of Majesty as a patriotic duty to her country and the throne. When war broke out in 1914, Queen Mary thought of a plan to collect money for schemes of work for women unemployed on account of the hostilities and under her patronage the Work For Women Fund was launched. The money collected was to be used to initiate and at first subsidise sensible business-like projects for employing women. Through this Fund, she became very friendly with a fiery woman radical, Mary MacArthur, who had organised the Sweated Industries Exhibition of 1906 which Queen Mary, then Princess of

Wales, had insisted on visiting. This had brought home to her the wretched condition of women who, in Edwardian days, were still being paid three farthings an hour for intricate sewing work, of the women chain makers who worked a 50-hour week at their own back yard forges for seven shillings a week. Mary MacArthur had successfully fought the established men's Trade Union on behalf of her own Women's Trade Union League. In 1914, she had married Will Anderson who that year was elected Chairman of the Labour Party. Feeling that in time of war all shades of political opinion should be represented on the 'Work For Women' plan, Queen Mary despite advice to the contrary invited Mary MacArthur to see her at Buckingham Palace. The result of this meeting was remarkable. Both women recognised each other's qualities instinctively and became firm friends. "The Queen does understand and grasp the situation from the Trade Union point of view," Mary MacArthur told a colleague after one of her many subsequent audiences at Buckingham Palace. "I positively lectured the Queen on the inequality in the classes and the injustice of it. I feared I talked too much again," she related of another audience. Queen Mary listened carefully to all Mary MacArthur had to tell and she asked for a list of books on the serious social topics they discussed. The Queen not only took an intense interest in the decisions of her Central Committee but frequently went to look at the practical results achieved.

At the end of the war, the Queen would have liked Mary MacArthur to be rewarded in the Honours List, but the Government refused to do so on account of Mr. Anderson's very radical speeches during the Coupon Election Campaign.

Queen Mary's daily life in the 1920's was run with the precision of a well-made clock. She would be called at 7.15. At 9.00 the King and Queen had breakfast together. At 9.30 a bell would summon the lady-in-waiting currently on duty to the Queen's sitting-room where she would find her upright at her desk, a stack of open letters before her. The Queen had inherited from her mother the habit of herself opening every letter addressed to her personally, but unlike the Duchess of Teck, she dealt with these immediately with a quiet efficient speed, marking deserving cases with the initials of some appropriate charity with which she had influence. Unlike Queen Alexandra who was reputed to send a £5 note to anyone who wrote to her asking for help, Queen Mary judiciously assessed the sincerity of the writing by studying each letter. She rejected those which did not seem genuine and, on investigation, her instincts were usually proved to have been correct. She could also recognise on an envelope handwriting of which she might once have seen one specimen many years before. "Oh, yes, I thought I knew that handwriting," she would say with satisfaction for she was proud of her excellent memory. The Queen would next deal carefully with her correspondence, and when this was completed she would interview her Private Secretary. The remainder of the morning she spent alone in her room, writing and working until luncheon which, like breakfast, was shared with the King. At both meals, King George's parrot Charlotte would attend – a temperamental bird with quite violent language. In the afternoon, provided she had no public or charitable duty to perform, Queen Mary would go shopping or visit some gallery. Before dinner, she would rest, her lady-in-waiting reading aloud to her, while she herself did embroidery, and unless some member of the family were invited, she would dine alone with the King who would usually have to work at his despatch boxes.

King George V had pronounced views on women's clothing. Wives should stay as they were when they were first married. Any variation was tantamount to cheating on the men who selected them in a certain guise. Queen Mary had in her early days experimented with large summer hats, but the opposition from George had been so continuous that she ceased doing so. Lady Airlie, her lady-in-waiting for many years, has written that Queen

Mary was ever generous in her praise of other women: "In all the years of our friendship I never once saw a trace of feminine jealousy or spite in her. She had always been very much admired at court balls. She was actually not beautiful. She could at times, however, convey the impression of beauty almost more than any woman I have ever known, especially in evening dress. For then, the radiant quality was most apparent. The line of her neck and shoulders was flawless and her skin, which was like alabaster, was set off by her magnificent jewellery. In reality she was the least self assertive of women, essentially feminine. She had far more originality of mind than her husband and their views on current topics often differed widely. But when he contradicted her, she never argued with him or tried to press the point as most women would. She never even wore a colour which the King did not like. Her style of dressing was dictated by his conservative prejudice. She was much more interested in fashion than most people imagined, and sometimes I think longed to get away from the hats and dresses which were always associated with her."

Lady Airlie goes on: "Having been gifted with perfect legs, she once tentatively suggested to me in the 1920's that we might shorten our skirts a modest two or three inches, but we lacked the courage to do it until I ventured to be the guinea pig. I appeared at Windsor one day in a slightly shorter dress than usual. The plan being that if King George made no unfavourable comment, the Queen would follow my example. The next morning I had to report failure. The King on being asked whether he liked my new dress had replied decisively that he did not as it was too short. So I had my hem let down with all speed and the Queen remained faithful to her long full dresses."

Lady Airlie describes her last visit in November 1952, long after King George had died, to Queen Mary in her bedroom at Marlborough House. "All the while I was conscious of the perfection of everything around her, the exquisitely embroidered soft lawn nightgown – the same as those she had worn in her youth – the nails delicately shaped and polished a pale pink – the immaculately arranged grey hair. Her face had still a gentle beauty of expression – no trace of hardness as so many faces have in old age – only resignation. As I kissed her hand before leaving her, I noticed the extreme softness of her skin."

In 1924 the British Empire Exhibition had been held at Wembley. One of the most popular sections of it was where Queen Mary's doll's house stood. It came into being through a suggestion of Princess Marie Louise who knew of Queen Mary's fondness for miniature *objets d'art*. She asked Sir Edward Lutyens to design a doll's house worthy of presentation to the Queen by a group of her friends and well-wishers. He agreed and decided that the miniature house should be decorated with pictures and furniture specifically made to scale by the leading painters and craftsmen of the day so that when finished, it would enable future generations to see how a King and Queen of England lived in the 20th century, and what authors, artists and others of merit there were during that reign. Queen Mary approved of this since it raised the house from the sphere of the fanciful to that of historic purpose.

The house was Georgian in period and built on four floors. It was designed to accommodate a family of persons six inches high. The dining room could hold a party of twelve who would eat off gold plates or off Royal Doulton. In the King's library the tiny bookshelves held 200 volumes, the size of postage stamps, each written by a contemporary author in his own hand, while minute portfolios bulged with 700 watercolours and drawings of the same size.

The Queen's Saloon was lined in rose-coloured silk and furnished in the style of the second half of the eighteenth century. The bed linen in the King and Queen's room took one lady 1,500 hours to weave. The bathroom had walls of ivory and shagreen, and floors of African marble and mother of pearl. Real water spurted from the taps. The kitchen stove was perfect in all its details and a tiny gramophone in the children's room played *God Save The King*. In the garage was a series of fine reproductions of the royal Daimlers.

The building and furnishing gave Queen Mary a great deal of pleasure. Only one thing caused controversy. The wine cellar contained tiny bottles preserving some of the finest vintages of wine. This led to temperance performers writing angry letters to *The Times*, especially as well as wine there were beers and whisky both in bottles and a plentiful supply of brandy and liqueurs – and at least soft drinks.

On the principal floor is the Queen's bedroom, one of the most beautiful apartments in the house. The tiny coved ceiling painted by Glyn Philpot represents Day and Night. Round the cove are masses of night clouds lit with gold by the setting sun, while in the flat ceiling panel we see as through a skylight the small fleecy white clouds and tranquil blue sky of morning.

The creation of a house such as this was the result of the pursuit of perfection in so many fields by a host of architects, artists, writers, musicians, craftsmen and work people. As well as being a wonderful toy and, as it were a domestic museum, it is also a social document of the times of the Great Queen who inspired its creation.

1924 also saw the first Labour government in Britain. King George V had never been class conscious. His whole aim was to help his new ministers. He was anxious, too, that they should not find their contacts with himself and his court in any degree embarrassing. It was here that he was helped enormously by Queen Mary who already knew several of his ministers' wives through war work. Her knowledge of the ideals of the Labour Party had been clarified by her talks with Mary MacArthur, and she attributed much of the social unrest of the 1920's to bad housing.

The years 1928, 1929 and 1930 were clouded ones for Queen Mary for during most of them King George V was seriously ill. Throughout this long period of desperate anxiety Queen Mary astonished her family by the self control and reserve she showed. In May 1930 there fell the 20th anniversary of his accession to the throne and he wrote to her: "I can never sufficiently express my deep gratitude to you, darling May, for the way you've helped me and stood by me in these difficult times." In 1935 came the Silver Jubilee. Then, on 20th January 1936, the King passed away. "I am broken-hearted," Queen Mary wrote at the beginning of her account of the King's death. "At five to twelve, my darling husband passed away. My children were angelic." No sooner was King George V dead, then Queen Mary in a gesture of historic importance took the hand of her eldest son in hers and, stooping, kissed it. The King who had been her husband was dead. The King who was her son lived on. All those who came to see Queen Mary privately at this time were profoundly moved by her courage and calm. The Archbishop of Canterbury, Dr. Lang, stated: "The sons were painfully upset – I suppose they had seldom seen death. It was the Queen, so marvellously self-controlled, who supported and strengthened them."

The first few months of the new reign saw little outward change in the widow's daily life. She continued living in Buckingham Palace where King Edward VIII set up a small office for himself, retaining York House as his temporary base, while his mother occupied herself in the sad task of sorting her late husband's papers and possessions. She also embarked on the redecoration of Marlborough House where she was going to live in the future after 26 years in the Palace. It was a task of some magnitude, for she had assembled a huge collection of *objets d'art* and souvenirs of the Royal Family. It took her 10 months to accomplish.

Regarding the sad events of King Edward VIII's short reign, Queen Mary looked upon his decision to abdicate with consternation and anger. She summarised her feelings very clearly in a letter she wrote to him 18 months later: "You asked me in your letter of 23rd June to write to you frankly about my true feelings with regard to the present position and this I will now do. You will remember how miserable I was when you informed me of your intended marriage and abdication and how I implored you not to do so for our sake and for the sake of the country. You did not seem able to take any point of view but your own. I do not think you ever realised the shock which the attitude you took caused your family and the whole nation. It seemed inconceivable to those who had made such sacrifices during the war that you, as their King, refused a lesser sacrifice. After all, throughout my life, I have put my country before anything else and I cannot change now."

By a 500 years old tradition no British Queen Dowager had ever attended the Coronation of her husband's successor to the throne. Queen Mary believed that it would add to the sense of solidarity with which the whole royal family faced the reign of King George VI if she were present to witness the Coronation of her husband's successor in Westminster Abbey, and also if she herself took part in the Coronation procession through the streets of London. So she asked King George VI's permission, which was granted.

This inspired idea of Queen Mary was rewarded by a spontaneous demonstration of affection from the crowds. Obviously moved by this, she smiled and waved back again and again.

From the very beginning of the new reign, the old lady's advice proved invaluable to the new King and Queen who were courageously shouldering the unwanted load of sovereignty. Fourteen days after the Coronation, Queen Mary celebrated her 70th birthday. She enjoyed the glorious summer weather of that year, attending every court function, went to the Derby, the

Aldershot Tattoo, Wimbledon, and initiated a system of taking the new Heir Apparent to the throne, Princess Elizabeth, on educational expeditions to the Tower of London, the House of Commons, Greenwich, and other places of interest. All she did was aimed at reviving the nation's support for the Monarchy. When the Second World War broke out in 1939, Queen Mary left London at the Government's request and went to live at Badminton, the Duke of Beaufort's home in the West of England. Lady Mary Beaufort wrote to a friend that Queen Mary's servants who, up to then, had been pampered by her now "revolted and scorned our humble home. They refused to use the excellent rooms assigned to them. Fearful rows and battles were fought over my body – but I won in the end and reduced them to tears and pulp. I can laugh now but I have never been so angry. The Queen, quite unconscious of the stir, has settled in well and is busy cutting down trees and tearing down ivy."

Queen Mary stayed at Badminton for five whole years during which time no mention was allowed to be made to the Press of where she was in case the Germans should get to know. She spoke foreign languages with ease and care for their idiom and when she listened to a broadcast by Hitler her comment was: "What abominable German he speaks!" She was very courageous and only had one fear that of being kidnapped by the Nazis. She made arrangements for a plane to take her away from Badminton to a secret destination should a German landing occur. She always had three suitcases packed ready in case of such trouble. She kept one for herself and gave her two dressers, one each to guard. If an alert sounded it was also their duty to pack a full suitcase, filling it with tiaras and other jewels. This her ladies-in-waiting was to take with them.

Queen Mary actively supported the wartime campaign to collect scrap. It appealed to her belief in domestic economy and tidiness. Should she find a piece of bone, an old bottle, or a bit of iron, she would at once hand it to a somewhat reluctant lady-in-waiting to take home. One afternoon, she returned to the house dragging triumphantly behind her a large piece of iron to add to her collection. A few minutes later, however, a page brought her an urgent message: "Please, your Majesty, a Mr. Hodge has arrived and he says you have taken his plough and would you give it back to him please at once as he can't get on without it."

Queen Mary disapproved of ivy because she said it collected dirt and she was always recommending that it be torn down from the wooded strip, some ten miles in length which ran round the edge of the park at Badminton. Every day she would spend up to three hours, supervising the gathering of twigs and fallen branches. Unfortunately, as soon as part of it was clear, a storm would undo all their good work. When once staying at Harewood House in Yorkshire, she arranged to be motored down to Renishaw, Sir Osbert Sitwell's home. He was in a quandary as not all the furnishings were in good repair. So as to leave as little time as possible for her to notice these defects, he told his agent to cut all the ivy he could find on the estate and hang it over the stables so that it could easily be removed without stubbing their nails. Then before taking the Queen into the house, he showed her first the stables and, as he had hoped, it proved an irresistible temptation and they readily fell in with her suggestion that they would strip the ivy away. Sir Osbert insisted that the task should be thoroughly completed, which pleased the Queen. As the result, the work was far from completed when it was time for her to motor back for dinner at Harewood, so she could only hurriedly be shown the one well kept room in the house into which all the best pieces of furniture had been moved.

Later, King George VI heard about this when Sitwell was dining alone with him. "You know my mother once gave me and Lillibet ivy poisoning by making us pick it off walls at Sandringham," the King revealed.

Everything had to be perfect for Queen Mary. On another occasion, the wife of the owner of Polesden Lacey, Mrs. Greville, on hearing of a proposed afternoon visit by Queen Mary rushed up to London and returned with 24 small deer-skin rugs and when her husband asked why she replied: "I've brought them to cover up the holes in the carpet or Queen Mary will discover them with the end of her umbrella which is like a divining rod for such things."

Dinner at Badminton during the war was at 8.30 and Queen Mary would usually wear a sequined dress with an ostrich-feather cape and several rows of pearls but no jewels. The food was good but strictly austere, and to save washing up, an oilcloth tablecloth patterned to look like linen was used. The meal would be over by nine when the radio was switched on and Queen Mary and her lady-in-waiting would whip out their knitting for, during a war, more even than during peace, no moment must be idle. When the Duke of Beaufort was on leave from his regiment, he was compelled by Queen Mary to knit a scarf on a wooden frame of pegs during his post-prandial moments.

Sir Osbert Sitwell relates how in September 1939 he had accompanied Queen Mary in her car to various engagements in and near Bath when they drove past a large building in a wooded park, and the Queen remarked: "How interesting, that must be the School for the Orphan Daughters of Officers that my Mother used to take such an interest in!" At that moment children carrying hockey-sticks appeared and stared in a desultory adenoidal way at the large royal motor and its august occupant. As Queen Mary passed the girls, she smiled at them but they merely stood still mooning vacantly at her. And then Sir Osbert heard Queen Mary observe to herself: "*Cheer* little idiots, can't you?"

Queen Mary encouraged the romance between Lillibet and Prince Philip when other members of the Royal Family were doubtful. One member was injudicious enough to make fun of Prince Philip's upbringing years as he put it at: "A crank school with theories of complete social equality where the boys were taught to mix with all and sundry." Would this sort of background for a son-in-law prove useful or baleful? Queen Mary bestowed upon the questioner one of her most withering looks. "Useful," she said shortly. She was delighted when the engagement took place. At an evening party at Buckingham Palace attended by most of the remaining European Royalty, Queen Mary was present and wrote in her diary: "Saw many old friends. I stood from 9.30 till 12.15am. Not bad for a someone aged 80." Lady Airlie who accompanied her wrote that she looked supremely happy and continued: "When Winston Churchill went up to greet her she held out both hands to him – a thing I never knew her to do before."

It was on Tuesday, 24th March 1953, at 10.20 in the evening that Queen Mary passed away whilst sleeping peacefully, and so two months short of her 86th birthday – a year after the death of her second son, King George VI – ended the long life of Queen Mary – a life spent in such a way as to earn her the respect of billions of her subjects. A single wreath of sweet-scented spring flowers with the inscription: "To Grandma England. In loving memory from her devoted Lillibet and Philip" surmounted her coffin as, draped with her personal standard, it was borne through the streets of London from Marlborough House to Westminster Hall for the lying-in state on Sunday, March 29th. One hundred and twenty thousand people filed through to pay their respects.

One of Queen Mary's ladies-in-meeting once said of her: "It was not only that she attracted people of character. It was more than that. No one could be near her without developing character. No one could serve her without growing. One realised slowly that only the best was good enough for her and she inspired one to grow in capacity and to give the best in return."

George VI and Elizabeth of Glamis

The Duke of Windsor related in his memoirs that the only time he and his brothers and sister were really happy as children was when they were with their mother in the early evenings. Their father, the future King George V, they rarely saw. Then one morning in spring 1902 at their London home, York House, the Duke recalled that he and his second brother, christened Albert Frederick Arthur George, but known in the family as 'Bertie', heard father stamping up the stairs. In some apprehension they watched the door. When this opened, it revealed a gaunt stranger with a large moustache standing next to their father who snapped: "This is Mr. Hansell, your tutor." And with that he walked out of the room. For highly-strung Bertie removal from the nursery to the schoolroom was far worse than for his less inhibited brother and sister. Bertie himself was generally blamed for any misdemeanour by the trio and summoned to father's room. Due to the latter's intimidating sternness Bertie developed the stammer which was to torment him for the rest of his life. He had also been born left-handed and was forced to write with his right-hand. The treatment he received from his father made the condition worse. Also, he suffered from knock-knees, and from the age of eight was forced to wear a set of splints on his legs for several hours during the day and to sleep in them at night. Possibly, because of this cruel treatment, Prince Albert grew up with straight legs, but the psychological effect of being compelled to wear splints can only have made life a torment for a boy who already had a stammer to cope with.

In January 1907 Prince Edward began his first term as a cadet at the Royal Naval College, Osborne, and two years later Prince Albert, just aged thirteen, arrived there accompanied by Hansell, his tutor, whose report read:

"I can state as a fact that he has reached a good standard all round, but we must remember that he is at present a 'scatter-brain' and it is perfectly impossible to say how he will fare at Osborne under the influence of all the excitement attendant on the new life... Like his brother he cannot get on without a 'bit of a shove' and, after our experience of Prince Edward's first two terms, I do hope that he will not be left too much to himself. At present they must have a certain amount of individual help and encouragement, especially encouragement; a too literal interpretation of the direction that they are to be treated exactly the same as other boys, who have had three or four years at private school, must lead to disaster... He requires a firm hand, but in that respect the excellent discipline of Osborne will be just what he requires. I have always found him a very straightforward and honourable boy, very kind-hearted and generous. He is sure to be popular with the other boys."

The college was housed in the stable block of Osborne House, the huge villa on the Isle of Wight in which Queen Victoria had died just eight years previously. King Edward VII had refused to occupy it and in defiance of his mother's will had given it to the nation to be used as a convalescent home for officers while the stable block was to be turned into a preparatory training college for naval cadets. Prince Albert had to sleep on a hard bed in a dormitory in a temporary building made of asbestos sprinkled with sand which had already deteriorated so much that the boys could stick their feet through the walls. Everything was done at the double; cadets had to run everywhere. Albert learnt from his elder brother that the other boys had pushed his head through a classroom window and had then banged the sash down on his neck in a crude enactment of the decapitation of their ancestor, Charles I. He himself being then small and fragile in physique was nicknamed 'Sardine'.

King George V as the boys grew up had taken more interest in them and especially in Prince Albert's case because he was a natural athlete, an excellent horseman, golfer and skater. Osborne was basically a technical school but when attending classes in mathematics he sometimes would have to remain silent because his stammer stopped him from pronouncing the 'f' of the word, fraction. In the examination lists he is shown as either bottom or near it. His father wrote: "My dearest Bertie, I am sorry to say that the last reports from Mr. Watt with regard to your work are not at all satisfactory. He says you don't seem to take your work seriously, nor do you appear to be very keen about it. My dear boy, this will not do, if you go on like this, you will be at the bottom of your Term, you are now 71st & you won't pass your examination... if you don't take care."

But such warnings were fruitless. In the final examination, Bertie cane bottom. Nevertheless, in January 1911, he went on to the second stage of his naval education at Dartmouth Royal Naval college. In May 1910 King Edward VII had died and Bertie's father became King George V. On 11th September 1913, Prince Albert received his first commission as midshipman on the battle-ship, HMS *Collingwood*, but being liable to sea sickness he did not share his father's passion for sailing, and after visiting his elder brother at Magdalen College, Oxford, he confided to his mother, Queen Mary, that he wished he had been there rather than at sea. When war broke out, the *Collingwood* with the other battleships of the Fleet lay at Scapa Flow guarding the northern entrance to the North Sea. In Buckingham Palace, King George V wrote in his diary: "Please God that it will soon be over & that he will protect dear Bertie's life." Three weeks later the Prince was taken violently ill and was rushed to hospital to have his appendix removed. A semi-invalid at nineteen, Prince Albert was now to spend some miserable years in and out of hospitals or convalescing while his contemporaries fought and died. In February 1915 he did get back to the Collingwood, but not for long. Indigestion returned in various forms. He was sick every time he swallowed any food. They found that he was suffering from stomach ulcers. Anxiety over his father's health made his condition worse. The King's horse, alarmed by the sudden noise of close gunfire, reared up and fell over backwards on top of the King who was severely injured, fracturing his pelvis. Concern for him aggravated Albert's ulcer. He now loved his father deeply. They had grown close since he had left Dartmouth. George V's letters showed tenderness and understanding – and when they were together alone his second son helped him to deal with the contents of dispatch boxes from Ministers. The old King liked him best of all his children, and said later: "Bertie has more guts than the rest of them put together."

After a year at Trinity College, Cambridge, the Prince spent most of his time living at Buckingham Palace with his sister, Princess Mary, who busied herself performing public duties, inspecting Girl Guides and attending charity bazaars. Then she became engaged to Viscount Lascelles, the Earl of Harewood's heir, whom she married in February 1922 leaving Bertie as the sole occupant of the upper floor rooms at the Palace. On 21st March 1919 he had become the first President of the Boys' Welfare Association for those working in industry. His assiduity in visiting mines, factories and shipyards earned for him the nickname of the 'Foreman'. This led to the annual Duke of York's Camps of which the first was held in August 1921. The Duke personally invited 400 selected boys, half from public schools and the rest from members' firms to be his guests for a week in August at an annual summer camp.

The experiment was a great success. It was carefully prepared to ensure that class difference was avoided. Everyone wore shirts and shorts including the Prince himself who took part in the camp activities and liked to lead the singing and miming of *'Under the Spreading Chestnut Tree'*. These camps received tremendous publicity, presenting an image of caring royalty.

There can be no doubt that Bertie owed much to his wife christened 'Elizabeth Angela Marguerite Bowes Lyon' and the ninth of the ten children born two weeks prematurely on 4th August 1900 to Claude and Cecilia Bowes Lyon. Her father, Lord Glamis, allowed seven weeks to pass before he drove into Hitchin from his estate, St. Paul's, Walden Bury, in Hertfordshire, to register the birth. In 1904 he became the 14th Earl of Strathmore. He was deeply conscious of his heritage, scrupulous in the discharge of all responsibilities. The little girl's mother was the daughter of a clergyman and it was from her that she inherited a zest for life and a flawless complexion. She learned that she was descended from King Robert the Bruce, hero of the Scottish War of Independence.

During the First World War, Elizabeth helped to nurse soldiers at Glamis which became a hospital for wounded servicemen. One of her brothers, Fergus, who served in the Black Watch, was killed at Loos, and three more were wounded at the front. She told Lady Cynthia Asquith: "Lessons were neglected for during those first few months we were so busy knitting, knitting, knitting and making shirts for the local battalion, the 5th Black Watch. My chief occupation was crumpling up tissue paper until it was so soft that it no longer crackled to put into the lining of sleeping-bags."

In December 1914, the first wounded soldiers arrived and were comfortably placed in the dining-room which had been turned into a ward. Lady Strathmore stressed that the men were to be treated as "honoured guests". Unlike other hospitals, there were no rules and restrictions. This was the first Christmas that Elizabeth had ever spent at Glamis. There were twenty wounded soldiers in the ward. They now became the centre in the lives of Elizabeth and her mother. One sergeant said: "My three weeks at Glamis have been the happiest I ever struck. I loved Lady Strathmore so much on account of her being like my dear mother, and as for Lady Elizabeth, why she and my 'fiansay' are as like as two peas."

Those who could walk took their meals in the crypt. In fine weather, the servicemen explored the grounds or were taken for picnics in the hills. Indoors, they took over the billiards room, and would gather there whenever they liked despite the precious and faded frail tapestries. They would stand around the piano for sing-songs. Elizabeth's favourite contribution was *'Strawberry Fair'* which always won for her hearty applause. Sometimes she helped with the composition of the patients' letters home.

One of the future Queen's regular chores was to run the mile up to the village to buy tobacco, cigarettes, and sweets. On cold dark evenings without, when logs blazed up the chimney, small tables were drawn up and rubbers of whist played by the soldiers in which Lady Elizabeth would take part.

Sergeant Pearne, wounded in August 1915 and left with a shattered shoulder, has related how he first encountered Lady Elizabeth soon after arrival when he happened to wander into King Duncan's chamber. "There I suddenly came face to face with a huge brown bear, stuffed and standing on its hind legs with its mouth wide open. I got a rare fright and must have shown it, because the next thing I heard was someone roaring with laughter. Looking up, I saw a cheeky little face at the window. Feeling a fool, I glowered at her. It was only later that I discovered who she was."

Letters from troops once convalescent at Glamis reveal Elizabeth's skill at poker games and ask how she is faring with the Red Queen.

There was another side to life at Glamis for Elizabeth during those early years. Sergeant Pearne recalled the daily sight of her dainty figure anxiously awaiting the arrival of the postman. "She always rose early and stood in the same place looking down the drive. With so many friends and relations at the front, she wanted to be the first to know what had happened so that she could look after her mother." Sadly, Elizabeth's vigil paid off. In late September 1915 the dreaded black edged telegram arrived. Fergus leading his men had been killed. Then a year after his death, a fire broke out at the top of the Castle's ancient central keep and Elizabeth took a leading part in trying to extinguish the blaze and in saving her ancestral home from being razed to the ground. The report in the *Dundee Courier* called her "a veritable little heroine" in the salvage work she performed within the fire zone.

Further news came the following year when two of her brothers were badly wounded, and on April 28th, 1917, Michael seven years older than Elizabeth whom she had regarded as her mentor and protector was reported missing, presumed dead.

David, the Strathmore's tenth child and Elizabeth's younger brother, was summoned home from Eton. The family went into mourning, but the boy famous for having second sight refused to do so, saying that he had seen Michael twice. "He is in a big house, surrounded by fir trees. I think he is very ill, because his head is tied up in a cloth." David was proved right, Michael had been taken prisoner by the Germans.

On Derby night 1920 King George V gave his annual dinner at Buckingham Palace to the members of the Jockey Club, while Queen Mary and the Princes dined at Lady Farquhar's house, 7 Grosvenor Square, before a ball which took place later in the evening. Among the dancers was nineteen-year-old Lady Elizabeth Bowes Lyon. It was not apparently the first time Prince Albert had met her for years earlier at a children's party given by Lady Leicester, Elizabeth when only aged five and dressed in a long blue and white dress with a floppy bow in her hair, is said to have presented the ten-year-old Prince with a cherry off her cake.

This was an early instance of the future Queen's famous ability to make friends with a charming gesture, and also a childish act of self-sacrifice for she always had a sweet tooth. At the Farquhars' ball Prince Albert saw her talking to his equerry, James Stuart, went up to him and said: "Who was that lovely girl you were talking to? Introduce me to her." It seems that Lady Elizabeth's affect on her future husband was immediate; he confessed to Lady Airlie later that he had fallen in love with her, although unconsciously that evening.

Lady Elizabeth was short, about 5' 4" tall, with a dazzling complexion, vivid blue eyes in a heart-shaped face and dark hair cut in an unfashionable fringe. Her clothes were old fashioned. Lady Airlie, who knew her well, wrote that she was unlike the cocktail-drinking, chain-smoking girls who came to be regarded as typical of the 1920's. She added: "Her radiant vitality and a blending of kindness and sincerity made her irresistible to men." Bertie began taking every opportunity to see her both in London and in Scotland. His sister Princess Mary had become a close friend of hers through their mutual work for the Girl Guide Movement – Lady Elizabeth was District Commissioner for Glamis. It was thanks to Princess Mary that she was first invited to Buckingham Palace.

Having discovered from conversations with Bertie that he had fallen in love with Elizabeth Bowes Lyon, his mother, Queen Mary, paid a special visit to Glamis to inspect her and thoroughly approved of the girl. The Queen discussed the matter with her life-long friend and lady-in-waiting, Mabell, the Countess of Airlie. Soon after this the Duke and Lady Elizabeth started dropping in at Lady Airlie's London flat on various pretexts, always separately. Lady Airlie wrote: "She was frankly doubtful, uncertain of her feelings and afraid of the public life which would lie ahead of her as the King's daughter-in-law. The Duke's humility was touching. He was deeply in love."

Encouraged by his mother and prodded by his elder brother, Bertie in the spring of 1921 proposed to Elizabeth. She refused. Lady Airlie wrote to Lady Strathmore: "The Duke looked so disconsolate. I do hope he will find a nice wife who will make him happy." Elizabeth's mother replied: "I like him so much, and he will be made or marred by his wife."

Despite all this, the young couple remained friends, meeting at the season's main events – Ascot and Henley, and in August for the shooting in the Highlands. Queen Mary instead of going abroad to visit her relations went first to Scotland to stay with Lady Airlie and then at Glamis. When Queen Mary's motor-car arrived there, Lady Elizabeth was waiting on the steps to greet her and by the time the Queen left she was certain that this was the one girl who could make Bertie happy.

In February, Princess Mary's wedding to Viscount Lascelles took place and among her bridesmaids was Elizabeth. Then that autumn, when attending another royal wedding in Belgrade, Bertie was irritated by a rumour that he was going to marry Lady Mary Cambridge.

Two months later Bertie accepted an invitation to shoot at Glamis. 'Chips' Channon was also there and wrote in his diary: "One rainy afternoon we were sitting about and I pretended I could read cards, and I told Elizabeth Lyon's fortune, and predicted a great and glamorous royal future. She laughed, for it was obvious that the Duke of York was much in love with her."

The following January, Channon wrote in his diary: "The evening papers have announced Elizabeth's engagement to the Prince of Wales. So we all bowed and bobbed and teased her, calling her, 'Ma'am'. I am not sure that she enjoyed it. It couldn't be true, but how delighted everyone would be! She certainly has something on her mind. She is more gentle, lovely and exquisite than any one alive, but this evening I thought her unhappy and distraite. I longed to tell her I would die for her, although I am not in love with her."

Eight days later out walking with Elizabeth in the woods, Bertie summoned up the courage to propose to her again, and he was overjoyed to be accepted. He sent a pre-arranged telegram to King George and Queen Mary saying simply: "All right, Bertie."

"Evelyn" wrote in *The Tatler*: "Aren't you thrilled and glad that the royal engagement is announced at last? Of course it had been rumoured and talked about for the last eighteen months or more, but nobody seemed quite to know whether it would or would not come off. Probably the two didn't know themselves. It is a big position with big responsibilities for a young girl who isn't of royal blood to have to face."

The wedding took place in Westminster Abbey on 26th April 1923. Among the 3,000 guests there were at the Duke's request 30 factory boys and another 20 who had attended his summer camps, and before walking up the aisle, the bride spontaneously laid her bouquet on the Tomb of the Unknown Warrior.

Prince Albert from his youth had been hampered when talking in public by his stammer, and, owing to the absence of his elder brother, the Prince of Wales, abroad, he had to make the closing speech on 31st October 1925 at the British Empire Exhibition. It was a tremendous ordeal for him. The Stadium had the largest arena in the country and the microphone would be relaying his words not only to the thousands present but also to a world-wide ten million people. His father, King George V, had made the speech opening the Exhibition a year previously and was bound to be critical, so Albert wrote to him revealing his worries and saying: "I shall be very frightened as you have never heard me speak and the loud-speakers are apt to put me off as well. So I hope you will understand I am bound to be more nervous than I usually am." It was the worst ordeal of his life so far. Here and there no sound came as he struggled to form the words. To his family and in fact to all who listened to him, the speech appeared to show that he was unfit for public life.

In the audience at Wembley on 31st October listening to the Duke of York's painful, hesitant words was an Australian speech therapist, Lionel Logue who commented to his son: "He's too old for me to manage a complete cure. But I could very nearly do it. I'm sure of that." Logue's experience had arisen through caring for shell-shocked ex-service men who had suffered from speech problems after the First World War. This eventually led to Prince Albert's visiting Logue on 19th October 1926 in his Harley Street consulting-room.

Sir John Wheeler-Bennett in his official biography of King George VI wrote later that the Prince's near despair had been cause by the failure of previous specialists to effect a cure. This had begun to breed within him the "inconsolable despair of the chronic stammerer and the secret dread that the hidden root of the affliction lay in the mind rather than in the body".

Logue used a two-pronged method of treating the Prince by convincing him that he could be cured through his own efforts and that he was a perfectly normal individual with a curable complaint. Logue concentrated on relaxing the tension which caused the muscles to spasm and prevented speech from flowing by teaching George to breathe correctly, to develop his lungs through exercises and to control the rhythm of his diaphragm. George had to do these exercises at home for an hour every day lying on the floor, to gargle with warm water and to stand by an open window intoning the vowels in a fairly loud voice, each sound to last for fifteen seconds. Logue prepared tongue-twisters which included some of the consonants that the Prince found difficult but were so absurd that they made him laugh, such as: "She sifted seven thick-stalked thistles through strong thick sieves." Logue thought it essential that they should meet on equal terms because he regarded an easy personal relationship as part of the treatment. The weekly consultations were held at 146 Harley Street or at his small flat in South Kensington.

The Duchess of York was extremely interested in her husband's treatment and often accompanied him to Harley Street. In public he would always look to her for reassurance and her approving reactions would encourage him. When later as King he used to broadcast, she would always be present, helping him to prepare the speech, to cut out difficult consonants, and to rehearse. Her help was of enormous importance, but, according to Logue, the vital factors were George's own courage and determination to fight his private nightmare and overcome it. Logue later said of him: "He was the pluckiest and most determined patient I ever had."

The Duke of York wrote to his father, King George V: "I have been seeing Logue every day & I have noticed a great improvement in my talking & also in making speeches which I had to do this week. I am sure I am going to get quite all right in time, but twenty-four years of talking in the wrong way cannot be cured in a month. I wish I could have found him before, as now that I know the right way to breathe, my fear of talking will vanish."

On 6th January 1927, the Yorks left for their first major tour abroad. Its ultimate objective was to open the new Parliament Buildings at Canberra which had become the capital of the Commonwealth of Australia. On the 27th of that month the Duke wrote to Logue that for the first time in his life he could make a speech in public without any hesitation. He was supported enormously throughout by his wife whose radiant personal charm cloaked his shyness. They began New Zealand where they triumphed. Then in Christchurch she was taken ill with tonsillitis leaving him unsupported by her. He was deeply worried and considered ending the tour and going back to Wellington. But the authorities were extremely upset and pointed out how disappointed the people would be, so he battled on without her and success strengthened his new confidence.

From Melbourne in Australia he wrote to Logue telling him how he had received a standing ovation from thousands of ex-serviceman on Anzac Day. Then in Canberra on 9th May after opening the door of the new Parliament House, instead of just doing this while the Royal Proclamation was read out by someone else, he made a speech before 20,000 people. In fact he went on making speech after speech. Inside the building despite the temperature reaching 80 degrees caused by the arc lights set up for the camera-men, the future King George VI gave his address from the throne without any hesitation. He wrote to his father: "I was not nervous when I made the speech, because the one I made outside went off without a hitch, & I did not hesitate once. I was so relieved as making speeches still rather frightens me, though Logue's teaching has really done wonders for me as I now know how to prevent & get over any difficulty. I have so much more confidence in myself, which I am sure comes from being able to speak properly at last."

Sir Tom Bridges, Governor of South Australia, wrote to King George V: "His Royal Highness touched people profoundly by his youth, his simplicity and natural bearing, while the Duchess has left us with the responsibility of having a whole continent in love with her. The visit has done untold good and has certainly put back the clock of disunion and disloyalty 25 years as far as this State is concerned."

King George V was delighted with the success of the visit. Back at Balmoral in September that year, the Duke of York could at the age of thirty-one actually make his father listen to him at last and he wrote to Logue that he did not have to repeat every-thing. The King wrote to Queen Mary later from Sandringham: "Delighted to have Bertie with me yesterday evening. I have had several talks with him and find him very sensible." The King added that Bertie was very different to the Prince of Wales whose private life was causing him increasing concern.

On returning from Australia in 1927, the Yorks lived in their London home at 45 Piccadilly, then from 1931, they were allotted by King George V a country home, the Royal Lodge in Windsor Great Park where Bertie became a keen gardener. At the 1947 Chelsea Flower Show, the first to be held after the Second World War, thanks to him it contained the finest display of rhododendrons in the show's history, and by the time of his death the gardens at the Royal Lodge had increased from 15 to 90 acres. Thanks to Logue, the Duke of York continued to make excellent progress with his speech making until the time of Edward VIII's abdication, when Dr. Lang, the Archbishop of Canterbury, interfered over the procedure for the Coronation Service.

He, Reith of the B.B.C., and the Duke of Norfolk, hereditary Earl Marshal in charge of royal occasions, agreed that the ceremony should be broadcast from Westminster Abbey for the first time, but turned down the B.B.C.'s proposal for televising it with the necessary apparatus on a small platform above the reredos, which would be camouflaged. On 13th January, Lang wrote in a memorandum:

"Inasmuch as the results of this television could only be seen by a limited number of people within about 25 miles of London who happened to have the necessary equipment in their houses, the Earl Marshal and I considered that it was not worthwhile to have television." Lang added in pencil: "No possibility of censuring."

This did not apply to filming, for the Archbishop and the Earl Marshal were to censor the film of the Coronation on the evening after it took place. Lang was worried that a live television broadcast might reveal incidents embarrassing to the King, who could suffer from muscular spasms in his cheeks and jaws when struggling to enunciate a word. It seems that Lang recommended a new speech therapist to prepare the King for the ordeal. But Lord Dawson, the King's chief medical advisor, wrote back on 25th March: "I consider any such change inadvisable seeing that the King has considerable confidence in Logue. For myself I think it is quite likely that the King will begin practising his broadcast while he is at Windsor for Easter. He thinks so himself and has suggested that Logue, whom he knows well should be with him."

A month later on 25th April Lang wrote in another memorandum that he and Assistant Private Secretary, Clive Wigram, had agreed not to let anyone but Logue see the King because "it would only increase his self-consciousness and nervousness".

Reith instructed Robert Wood, the B.B.C.'s engineer in charge of outside broadcasts, to make "a good broadcaster of the King". Wood, a microphone expert, was to help him minimise the effects of his stammer. Wood began rehearsals with the King standing at a high ledger desk because Logue believed that standing made him speak more clearly. Wood wrote in his memoirs: "Little by little I helped him with tone and lip formation and showed him how he could let the microphone do the work… He eventually became a master of the microphone and a very good broadcaster. At the beginning, however, his delivery tended to be monotonous; he spoke slowly and carefully with a rhythmic emphasis developed to carry him along in breathing phases with pauses." Logue called them three-word breaks in between, and there was always the lurking fear that he would stop. Logue goes on: "There was something touching about hearing that manly voice hesitate and then go doggedly on, even forcing himself sometimes to repeat words two or three times in order to be able to carry on."

Normally Logue and Wood would go carefully through the script checking words that might trip the King up. His chief problem was with initial 'c's and 'g's. Wood says that, later during the War, words with double 's's like 'oppression' and 'suppression' which were used quite often gave him trouble. "But the King struggled without let up. I was full of admiration for his perseverance."

The Coronation was full of hazards. The words of the service were fixed by tradition and could not be changed. The Queen's presence helped enormously and Logue was in charge. On 5th May the King read his whole speech. It was recorded and played back. The royal couple with Logue and Reith listened to the first attempt in the King's bedroom. Reith wrote: "There were a good many stutters so we tried again." But when it came to doing it live, the King got through much better than at rehearsals, and as *Time* magazine afterwards reported: "It was a triumph." The King said: "It is with a very full heart I speak to you tonight. Never before has a newly-crowned King been able to talk to his peoples in their own homes on the day of his Coronation... The Queen and I will always keep within our hearts the inspiration of this day. May we ever be worthy of the goodwill which I am proud to think surrounds us at the outset of my reign."

Sarah Bradford wrote in her biography of King George VI that despite the long shadow of recent events and Edward VIII's abdication: "The Coronation ceremony was both beautiful and moving, its historical ritual obliterating the sad, sordid memories of recent months and elevating the idea of Kingship." Queen Victoria's grand-daughter Princess Alice, Countess of Athlone, thought that out of all the four Coronations she had attended: "Bertie's was the most moving." She added: "I thought Bertie looked too wonderful as he stood at the altar divested of his robes and wearing only knee breeches and a shirt which showed his fine figure."

The Coronation Oath read out by the Archbishop of Canterbury went: "Do you solemnly promise and swear to govern the peoples of Great Britain, Ireland, Canada, Australia, New Zealand, and the Union of South Africa, of your possessions and the other territories to them belonging or pertaining, and of your Empire of India, according to their respective laws and customs."

For Lionel Logue one of the great moments of his life was when the King looked at him sitting in the Royal Box and gave an imperceptible nod, as if to say: "We did it!"

The success of the Coronation led to great popular enthusiasm for the new King and Queen.

That autumn, the King delivered the speech from the throne at the State Opening of Parliament without a hitch. The Queen took over her new role with ease. She was a natural actress. One of her major advantages both as a woman and as a Queen was her ability to make anyone to whom she was speaking feel that person was the one person in the world to whom the Queen wanted to talk. She really gave the impression she was enjoying herself. "I find it hard to know when not to smile!" she admitted to Cecil Beaton.

In the summer of 1938 King George VI and Queen Elizabeth paid their first State Visit to Paris against a background of gathering war clouds. Even the Communist newspaper, *L'Humanité*, spoke warmly of them. *L'Illustration* magazine described Queen Elizabeth as descended from the Kings of Scotland who had given France as the wife of one of its Kings, *"la charmante Marie Stuart"*. It wrote of George VI: "The handshake he gives is frank and energetic with *je ne sais quoi* of spontaneity and sympathy and it puts you at once at your ease how ever modest your social station might be."

The Dowager Duchess of Rutland told Sarah Bradford how from the balcony above the staircase at the Opera she watched the King and Queen coming up preceded by two footmen carrying twenty-branched candelabrum of tall white candles, the King, slim and handsome, the Queen, radiant in diamonds and wearing the white Winterhalter crinoline designed for her by Hartnell. "Now I felt proud of my nation," said the Dowager Duchess. "The

French were mad about the King and Queen. Winston Churchill was like a schoolboy he was so delighted."

At Malmaison, two old ladies in tears begged Lady Diana Cooper for her place in the royal path. "You see her all the time," one said. "If only we had a King!" said the other.

On 1st September 1938, after the visit, the British *chargé d'affaires* in Paris, Ronald Campbell, wrote to Lord Halifax: "For the Queen the visit has been an heroic effort coming so soon after the death of her mother, the Countess of Strathmore."

One of the greatest services George VI and his Queen paid to Britain was through their visit to Canada in May, 1939. The weather was appalling as the *Empress of Australia* made its perilous way across the North Atlantic. The Queen wrote to her mother-in-law, Queen Mary: "The fog was so thick that it was like a white cloud round the ship, and the foghorn blew incessantly... We very nearly hit a berg the day before yesterday, and the poor Captain was nearly demented because some kind cheerful people kept on reminding him that it was about here that the *Titanic* was struck, & just about the same date." The King himself added: "I should not myself have chosen an ice field surrounded by dense fog in which to have a holiday, but it does seen to be the only place for me to rest in nowadays!"

On 17th May, the royal couple arrived in Quebec and became the first reigning British monarchs to set foot in the New World. The French-speaking crowds were impressed with the Queen. The tour became a triumph for the royal couple. The leader of the French nationalists said ruefully: "We might as well forget demanding independence for Quebec as the people here have turned madly Imperialist." At Ottawa, Lord Tweedsmuir, the Governor-General, wrote to Lord Hardinge describing what took place when the King unveiled the War Memorial. He had spoken admirably and clearly, as he had done every time since landing. The Queen after the ceremony said she wanted to go down among the veterans. They were absorbed in a crowd of nearly seven thousand. "It was a wonderful example of what a people's King means, and it would have been impossible anywhere else in the world. One old man shouted to me: 'Ay, man, if Hitler could see this!' It was extraordinarily moving because some of these old fellows were weeping." Tweedsmuir ended: "The capacity of Their Majesties for getting in touch with the people amounts to genius. It is the small unscheduled things that count most, and for these they have an infallible instinct."

In another letter Tweedsmuir wrote that the King was "a wonderful mixture of shrewdness, kindliness and humour" whilst the Queen had "a perfect genius for the right kind of publicity, the unrehearsed episodes which here were marvellous".

J.A. Stevenson, correspondent of *The Times*, wrote in a private letter to Geoffrey Dawson: "The royal tour has been an unqualified success from start to finish and their Majesties did a first-rate job and achieved a great personal triumph. If I had not seen it with my own eyes, I would not have believed that they could have evoked such demonstrations of loyalty and personal affection from a people normally so inarticulate and unemotional as the Canadians are. But they combined regal dignity in their public appearances with a democratic friendliness in their private contacts."

U.S. reporters covering the royal journey across Canada were enormously impressed by the King and Queen. George Dixon of the New York *Daily News* wrote: "British readers can have no idea of the punishment the royal couple endured on their gruelling trip, never with a chance to relax, always on parade... The King has a terrific sense of humour."

Mackenzie King, the Canadian Prime Minister, at the end of the visit in Victoria, British Columbia, cabled Tweedsmuir describing in rapturous terms the impressive and moving way the

King and Queen behaved throughout. Now if war did break out with Germany there could be no risk of Canada staying neutral.

The King and Queen's triumphant tour of Canada formed a propitious prelude to their first visit to the United States. The morning of 8th June 1939, saw them arrive at Washington Union Station to be welcomed by President Franklin Delano Roosevelt and his wife Eleanor. Some 60,000 people lined the route as they drove in an open carriage to the White House. Eleanor wrote later in *This I Remember* that her admiration for the Queen "grew every minute she spent with us" and added: "She did not cease to smile or, like the King, to do her duty with as much conscientiousness as good grace." According to *Time* the next day included a visit to the Capitol, where the King "endured an ordeal of Klieg lights and Congressional crudeness as 74 Senators and 352 Representatives trotted by in 25 minutes, while New York's Sol Bloom mispronounced their names and General George Patton addressed speeches of welcome to 'Cousin George' and 'Cousin Elizabeth'."

For the King the most fascinating part of the day was a visit to a Civilian Conservation camp. The boys were drawn up in two lines, the King stopping to speak to every other boy and the Queen to the intervening ones. Earlier, he had described to the Roosevelts, his own Duke of York's Camps for Boys in the depressed mining areas. On reaching the end of the second row, the Camp Commandant suggested that although the American boys had prepared their barracks and mess hall for inspection, the King might not feel up to crossing the field in the sweltering heat. George responded: "If they expect me to go, of course I will go." The Queen dutifully followed across the field with Mrs. Roosevelt where the King made a thorough inspection.

On the journey back to Washington, they paused at Arlington Cemetery, where the King laid a wreath by the Tomb of the Unknown Soldier and at the Canadian Cross, and then on for tea on the lawn of the White House – but not rest, for Mrs. Roosevelt had arranged this in response to the King's request to talk to all the heads of the government agencies activating national recovery under the New Deal. She had been told by Franklin that she must introduce every head to the King outlining the work they were doing and then give them three minutes with the King before taking them over to the Queen. Mrs. Roosevelt wrote: "I rather dreaded having to engineer this, and wondered how I was going to condense the introduction into a brief enough explanation, but I soon found that this could be very short, for the King seemed to know at once, as I spoke the name, what that person was doing, and he started right in with the questions. I was so impressed with the King's knowledge that I asked him later how he knew what work every person in the U.S. Government did. He told me that before he came, he had made a study of the names and occupations of everyone in the Government, that the material had been procured for him, and was part of his preparation for this trip to Washington."

The royal couple went next to New York where due to many of its people coming from races hostile to the British it was feared that they would be spurned. Fortunately, thanks to the highly favourable impression they had made since arriving in North America, quite the reverse occurred. "We like them – and we hope they us," declared the *New York World Telegram*. They were two great human beings who had won that distinction in their own right. The *New York Daily Mirror* witnessing their arrival at the Battery described the King and Queen as "a blondish, tired looking man who bowed stiffly" and "a cute, cuddly, home-looking girl in an ice-blue ensemble who beamed warmly". That smile "let loose the works. Wow! Zowie! Hey!" The crowds cheered and cheered loud enough to reach and resurrect the hated George III in his tomb back in Windsor as they drove with Mayor La Guardia to the World's Fair. The *New York Times* could recall "no parallel for the steady warmth of the greetings" from the largest crowds ever seen in the city.

The Queen had heard that the eight-year old daughter of Harry Hopkins, President Roosevelt's Secretary of Commerce, was disappointed that the King and Queen she saw did not look like those in fairy tales. To make up for this, the Queen arranged that the little girl be placed in a prominent position in the White House's hall when the royal couple left for a British Embassy banquet. As they passed close to the child, the Queen, shimmering with diamonds and wearing a tiara. Bent down and chatted to the child, who, delighted, turned to her father and exclaimed: "Daddy, oh Daddy, I have seen the Fairy Queen!"

On 12th June the *New York World Telegram* summed up: "We said we liked them much, when they came, and hoped they would like us. We like them even better after watching them take the hurdles of our hospitality."

Three days later, the King and Queen sailed for home aboard the *Empress of Britain*. George wrote: "I nearly cried at the end of my last speech in Canada, everyone round me was crying." Arthur Krock in the *New York Times* stated that the British sovereign had conquered Washington where they had not put a foot wrong and where they had left a better impression than even their most optimistic advisers could have expected.

The tour had a tonic effect on George himself improving his self-confidence and widening his knowledge of the world. He told an adviser from the Foreign Office: "There must be no more high-hat business, the sort of thing that my father and those of his day regarded as essential as the correct attitude – the feeling that certain things could not be done." Back in Britain, the royal couple received a wonderful welcome home. Along the railway line from Southampton to Waterloo were cheering people waving flags. When Parliament Square was reached, the bells of St. Margaret began to ring and, as Harold Nicolson wrote in his diary, even hardened M.P.'s "lost all dignity and yelled and yelled". His account continues: "The King wore a happy school-boy grin. The Queen was superb. She really does manage to convey to each individual in the crowd that he or she has had a personal greeting... She is in truth one of the most amazing Queens since Cleopatra. We returned to the House of Commons with lumps in our throats."

Sarah Bradford states in her excellent biography of the King that next day at the Guildhall "filled with new-found confidence and real emotion he made the best speech of his career so far". Sir Alan Lascelles, then his Assistant Private Secretary, wrote to Mackenzie King in Canada: "I have never heard the King – or indeed few other people – speak so effectively, or so movingly. Talking of British institutions founded on ideals of liberty and justice, of the Crown as head of a Commonwealth of Nations and a potent force for promoting peace and goodwill among mankind, the King obviously experienced such emotion that people felt he might break down, a feeling that made the speech even more effective."

The new reign had begun gloomily and then just as the King and Queen were beginning to feel secure, the Second World War broke out. Parents with sufficient means started sending their children out of London and large cities to safe havens in the country or to Canada and the United States. The two Princesses aged 13 and 9 were already living at Balmoral, so it was decided to leave them there for the time being. Meanwhile, a basement room at Buckingham Palace was converted into an air-raid shelter. The King and Queen toured the country, visiting army camps, munition factories, and the back streets of towns. Elizabeth's confidence and that ever present smile strengthened the morale of other women.

It was experiencing with the people of London the horrors of Hitler's Blitz on the capital in September 1940 that endeared King

George VI and his wife to them. On the clear night of the 7th to 8th, over 200 bombers killed more than 200 of the capital's people and seriously wounded 1,357 others. It was just the start and after 3 days the death toll had tripled. At first it was the working-class areas round the docks that suffered most. In the House of Commons, M.P.'s became worried about the bitterness that had arisen in the cruelly devastated East End. Then, fortunately, as Harold Nicolson put it from the point of view of the Ministry of Information, the German bombers started flattening the West End. On Friday 13th September, one made a direct hit on Buckingham Palace and the private chapel was destroyed. The King wrote in his diary how when he and the Queen were upstairs in his little sitting-room: "All of a sudden we heard an aircraft making a zooming noise above us, saw two bombs falling past the opposite side of the Palace, & then heard 2 resounding crashes as the bombs fell in the quadrangle about 30 yards away. We looked at each other, & then went out into the passage as fast as we could. The whole thing happened in a matter of seconds. We all wondered why we weren't dead. Two great craters had appeared in the courtyard. The one nearest the Palace had burst a fire hydrant & water was pouring through the broken windows in the passage. Six bombs had been dropped. The aircraft was seen coming down the Mall having dived through the clouds & had dropped 2 bombs in the forecourt, 2 in the quadrangle, 1 in the chapel & the other in the garden. There is no doubt that it was a direct attack on the Palace."

The King had had a narrow escape from death. The Queen bravely declared in public that now they were glad to be able to look the East End in the face. George VI was privately outraged at what he suspected to have been a deliberately planned attack upon himself. It suggested detailed local knowledge which Ribbentrop as former German Ambassador in London would have had. Only that July Ribbentrop had tried to mastermind kidnapping the Duke of Windsor from Portugal for the purpose of replacing George with his elder brother. Churchill's comment on the bombing was: "This shows the Germans mean business."

The bombing of Buckingham Palace had important propaganda merit entirely the reverse from that intended by Goering. King George wrote in his diary: "I feel that our tours of bombed areas in London are helping the people who have lost their relations and homes & we have found a new bond with them as Buckingham Palace has been bombed as well as their homes, & nobody is immune." *Time* magazine commented that the King spent a third of his working day visiting the blitzed parts of London and throughout the country. It added: "Never in British history has a monarch seen and talked to so many of his subjects or so shared their lives." The Minister of Food, Lord Woolton, went with the King and Queen and wrote in his diary for 11th October: "We motored through miles of streets in which all of the windows had been broken, doors blown off, and there were huge areas in which houses had been completely wrecked, arid it seemed to me impossible that anybody should live in these places again. The Queen asked me about the morale of the people who had been bombed, when we were coming through a very slummy district where a crowd gathered round the carriage and called out 'Good luck' and 'God bless you' and 'Thank you for coming to see us'. I knew the district and had been there only a week before. I said: 'You asked me about morale. All these people nave lost their homes.' The Queen was so touched she couldn't speak for a moment. I saw the tears come into her eyes and then she said: 'I think they're wonderful.' I was impressed by the way the King and Queen handled the situation – by the simplicity of both of them. They were so easy to talk to and to take round, and fell so readily into conversation with the people whom they were seeing, without any affectation or side. They were, in fact, very nice people doing a very human job."

As a result of these visits, the King was so moved that he decided to reward civilian gallantry with decorations equivalent to the Victoria Cross for servicemen in action. They were to be named the George Cross for conspicuous gallantry and the George Medal for devotion to duty among the Civil Defence Services and the civilian population as a whole. On the evening of 23rd September, the King announced the creation of these awards in one of his most memorable broadcasts. He said: "There will always be an England to stand before the world as the citadel of hope and freedom. Let us then put our trust, as I do, in God and, in the unconquerable spirit of the British people."

On 17th September the King with the Queen toured the sites of recently exploded land mines in Hendon, Wembley and Ealing. He was moved by the courage of the bomb disposal squads and furious with the petty-mindedness of the War Office in refusing them suitable rewards for their gallantry. David Euan Wallace, who accompanied him, wrote in his diary, now kept in the Bodleian Library, Oxford: "The King is very angry that the War Office will not recognise bomb disposal officers as being eligible for military decorations on the ground that they are not 'working in the face of the enemy'. He wanted to give Lt. Davies the V.C. and said some things about the Generals at the War Office that would have surprised them."

Lady Hambledon who often accompanied the Queen on these tours said later that the food was Spartan. "They were very ration-minded. I took a tin of old dog biscuits with me."

The King travelled over 52,000 miles of railway track to inspect men and women in the Services and key war industries and the victims of German bombing raids. Normally, he did this in the overhauled train which had once been used by Queen Victoria. When someone mentioned the possibility of an attack being made on him during such tours, he said: "Well, it's no use worrying because if someone wishes to kill me there's nothing to stop them. He found physical danger easier to endure than his private aversions such as fear of heights. Once he had to inspect a light-house. Rather than invent an excuse, he gritted his teeth and climbed to the top. Even when he had to review the guard in the quadrangle at Windsor he would get into a nervous state beforehand. The worst occasion was to be reviewing the Eighth Army troops in North Africa in the presence of Montgomery. When the time came for him to leave his tent, he suddenly muttered: "I can't – I can't! I'm not going to do it. I'm going home." Colonel Piers Legh said very quietly: "Well, all right, sir, but you'll have to swim." There was a tense pause, then suddenly the King smiled, seeing the humour of the situation. "Give me my cane," he said, rose and reviewed in a masterly way. Curiously, situations like this did not occur when the King was surrounded by crowds in bombed streets. There he found it easy to talk to people. On 25th August 1943, the King suffered a personal tragedy when his brother, the Duke of Kent, was in a Sunderland flying-boat on the way to Iceland to inspect R.A.F. installations. Flying too low through a dense mist, it hit the top of a hill and burst into a fireball.

The General Election of 1945 and the huge vote for Labour proved to be the equivalent of a Revolution without bloodshed. Nationalisation of coal, steel, the utilities, and the break up of the British Empire followed. Although George VI feared that the many changes were too sudden and drastic and might lead to economic chaos, Herbert Morrison was to write that he always found the King "fair in his observations and meticulously observant of the constitutional position".

In August 1947 when the Labour Government sought emergency powers, Churchill denounced this as a blank cheque for totalitarian government. The King then wrote to Attlee: "I need not say that I know very well that, so long as you are at the head of any government, due regard will be given to the rights of

Parliament itself, and that Parliament will be offered the opportunity of exercising its proper function... I know that your attitude towards this supremely important matter is the same as my own."

As Sarah Bradford points out in her biography of George IV, Attlee repaid the King's trust with an affection for him which he rarely demonstrated for any one else in his whole life. Brought to the throne in a climate of dynastic and constitutional crisis, George was to leave to his daughter a throne more stable than Britain had ever had.

Beaton's celebrated photograph of the Queen Mother at the Palace established a new romantic image for the Monarchy – that of an idyllic figure from a Victorian fairytale dressed in a shimmering crinoline decked with diamonds. He wrote: "In the daylight now she looked a dream... but what when the electric lamps were ablaze! They went on in a flash and to my utter amazement and joy the Queen looked even more of a dream – a porcelain doll – with a flawless little face like luminous china in front of a fire. Her smile as fresh as a dewdrop – her regard uncompromising and kindly – altogether a face that reveals what its owner is – someone with the best instincts – strict in her likes – sympathetic – witty – shrewd – wistful and so well-educated that she makes one full of admiration rather than shame. She is a great lady – an angel with genius – she makes every man feel she needs his protection though she can well get along on her own merits."

Alfred Wright, *Time*'s London correspondent, reporting on the opening of an exhibition of American art at the Tate Gallery by the King and Queen in June 1946 wrote: "Instinctively my attention was first attracted by the Queen. She has a superb complexion; everyone notices it right away. She moves with the unselfconscious ease of a person who knows she is alone and will not be disturbed. When someone is talking to her, she concentrates completely on what he or she is saying, despite any and all distractions. During the time I watched her, the Queen maintained a remarkable expression on her face – as if this was an experience she had been awaiting months, and it had turned out better than she had hoped."

Sarah Bradford in her biography of George VI comments: "This, the show business side of royalty, was the Queen's public role; in private she saw it was her duty to be supportive and protective of the King but she did not initiate policy or interfere in the political side of the King's affairs, nor did she make any attempt to make her own clique of courtiers."

The King left for South Africa in January 1947, a deeply tired man. The tour was an exhausting one, taxing even the Queen's formidable constitution. By January the following year he was already suffering from cramp in his legs and restriction in the flow of blood. The King made tremendous efforts, both physical and psychological, to bring himself back to health during the last year of his life. He was not told that he had cancer. He leaned, too, on his homeopathic doctor for remedies. His advisors, however, were already prepared for the worst. When, on 7th October, 1951 Princess Elizabeth and the Duke of Edinburgh finally took off on their tour of Canada and the United States, their original departure date had been put off because of the King's illness. The Princess's Private Secretary travelled with all the papers necessary for the Queen's formal accession if her father died while her she was abroad. Despite the King's illness the tour was a tremendous success. In Washington the couple stayed with the Trumans in the White House. The President wrote to the King: "We have just had a visit from a lovely young lady and her personable husband. They went to the hearts of all the citizens of the United States." The King was proud of his daughter's success and to mark it he sent his private train to meet them at Liverpool when the ship docked and made them both Privy Counsellors.

At Sandringham that Christmas the King seemed to be in excellent form. As ever Anglo-American relations were in the forefront of his mind and he was anxious to do personally all he could to help. The King now was making plans for a convalescent visit to South Africa. On 30th January he went up to London for a consultation with his doctors, who, apparently, pronounced themselves "well satisfied with their patient". The following evening, the Royal Family went to a performance of *South Pacific* at Drury Lane. It was in the nature of a family celebration of the King's recovery and also a last get-together before the Princess and the Duke flew off the following morning to undertake the tour of Australia and New Zealand originally planned for the King. The following day, 31st January, he went to Heathrow to see his daughter off to Kenya on the first stage of her journey. He stood hatless in the cold wind, his eyes with the glaring look they took on in moments of emotion. Churchill,who was present, described him as even jaunty. "But I think he knew he had not long to live."

On Wednesday 6th February, 1952 after a shoot at Sandingham, George retired early to bed. At some time during the night, he died peacefully in his sleep from coronary thrombosis. Far away in Nairobi Princess Elizabeth was watching wild life in the African bush. At 2.45 p.m. local time, 11.45 a.m. in London, the Duke of Edinburgh broke the sad news to his wife. This she bore with courage and calmness. When asked what name she would choose as Queen, she replied: "My own name – what else?"

Next day, the Prime Minister, Sir Winston Churchill, waited with a number of Privy Councillors at London Airport to receive Queen Elizabeth the Second. It was a sad young woman they watched come down the gangway from the plane. Fragile she may have looked but she had inner strength.

On Friday, 15th February, after some 400,000 people had paid their last respects to King George VI lying in state in Westminster

Hall, a gun carriage bearing the coffin took it to St. George's Chapel, Windsor, for the funeral.

In April, a Declaration was issued that the Royal Family's surname would in future be that of "Windsor".

One of the best tributes to King George VI following his death was sent by René Massagli, the French Ambassador in London, to Maurice Schuman, the Foreign Minister in Paris: "If the measure of a King lies in the manner in which his character and qualities correspond to the needs of a nation at a given moment in history then George VI was a great King, and perhaps a very great one. Courage, work and austerity have been the watchwords of the country for the last fifteen years and one could say that the King provided an example of them... He had to learn everything at the age of 41 on ascending the throne – and he learned quickly and well... By his simplicity, his goodwill, his courage, and his sense of duty, his respect for constitutional principles and the example of his private life, King George VI has amassed around the throne a capital of sympathy and loyalty upon which he could call in case of crisis. Brought to the throne in a climate of dynastic and constitutional crisis George VI has died leaving to his daughter, a throne more stable than England has known throughout almost her entire history."

Sarah Bradford ends her superbly researched biography by saying that among the wreaths was Churchill's final tribute to King George VI, one of white flowers bearing a note with two words in the old Prime Minister's hand: '*For Valour*'.

Queen Elizabeth II and her Family

S o what is it about monarchy that is beginning to appeal again? The alternative, an elective presidency, is proving less and less attractive as many of them cling to power. Also, corruption surrounding the election process is emerging, for example, Kohl in Germany; Mitterand and Chirac in France; the fiasco over the last American election, etc. The candidate for the presidency has not had a lifelong training for the job, and he is likely to be in a hurry to make his mark before his term of office is over, whereas a monarch is trained from birth for the job, does not have to divert his energy to seek re-election, so that he can concentrate on the long-term interests of the nation and build on what his forbears had started.

In the introduction to her book, *Royal Throne – The Future of the Monarchy*, first published in 1993, Elizabeth Longford described how, as the result of spending four years among Queen Victoria's family papers, she developed a firm belief in the monarchy's constitutional role and this gradually changed her from "an incipient republican to a firm monarchist". At the same time other experiences increased her royalist convictions. In 1989 meeting Prince Charles by chance, she congratulated him on his speeches of public interest and said that she hoped that he would continue to express his deeply felt convictions in a forthright manner, which was what was wanted of a Prince of Wales. He looked pleased as he walked away. Suddenly, he returned to say with a wry smile: "Yes, but I don't want to be thought of as some sort of freak!"

Elizabeth Longford relates how she was invited to the wedding of Princess Elizabeth and six years later to her Coronation. Each time she was impressed by the same thing: how serious, how absorbed, how carried out of herself she looked. "High seriousness is one of the Queen's greatest gifts."

Lady Longford ends her introduction by mentioning how the Queen called the year 1992 her *"annus horribilis"*. Yet in her Christmas message she made a point of ending on a heartening note. She had met the heroic Leonard Cheshire shortly before his death, and she saw him as the embodiment of what she herself passionately believed in: "Kindness in another's trouble, courage in your own."

In the film celebrating in 1992 the fortieth anniversary of her accession, the Queen said that she believed for a happy life people should take for their motto – "Moderation in all things." Elizabeth Longford lists the virtues fostered in a Queen who stands for moderation. First, admiration for order in the sense of system. Her governess, Marion Crawford, in *The Little Princess*, wrote how the future Queen would sometimes as a child get out of bed at night to make sure that her clothes were all neatly folded on her chair and her shoes in perfect order underneath. She was exceptionally calm. When an intruder burst into her bedroom at Buckingham Palace, she not only stayed calm, but kept him calm also, together with a pack of excitable corgis. She makes no hasty decisions. She goes for what matters, the essentials. "Take clothes. In her position, the main point is to be recognised. Fashion is irrelevant. Moderation rules out extravagance."

But in party politics, neutrality not moderation is required of her. Fortunately for the country, Queen Elizabeth II learnt this as a child from her father, King George VI.

In his book, *The Republic of Britain: 1760 to 2000*, the American historian, Frank Prochaska, reminds readers that many features of modern republicanism worldwide started in the United Kingdom. Not only was there an actual republic in England in the 17th century, but the English constitution, as it evolved from the

1680's until the 20th, provided a model followed round the globe. The British monarchy is the parent of non-executive presidencies wherever they are to be found. Even Tom Paine saw republicanism and monarchy as compatible. During Victoria's withdrawal from public life following the Prince Consort's death, anti-monarchism flourished and in 1864 a handbill appeared on Buckingham Palace's railings stating: "These extensive premises to be let or sold, the late occupant having retired from business." However, six years later, the trade union paper, *The Beehive*, stated: "As a matter of fact our government at the present time is in reality, though not in name, a republic with a hereditary President." By the end of the century Queen Victoria's death brought about, in Fabian Beatrice Webb's words, "a real debauch of sentiment and loyalty – a most impressive demonstration of the whole people in favour of the monarchical principle".

Prochaska calls the 1918 Representation of the People Act – "the jewel in the crowned republic" which cemented the monarchy into the democratic constitution. In 1917, the Socialist, Robert Blatchford, conceded: "I cannot see that it matters much what we call our ruler, so long as he does not rule." Six years later, the Labour Party voted 10 to 1 against a republic. Commenting on the cheering crowds celebrating King George V's 1935 Jubilee, George Orwell described "the survival of an idea almost as old as history, the idea of the King and the common people being a sort of alliance against the upper classes".

One of the most poisonous attacks on the Royal family was made in the early 1990's by the radical playwright David Hare who trumpeted: "We shall mock them till they wish they had never been born." Prochaska comments: "He is now *Sir* David."

Today nothing measures the value of the monarchy more than the daily variety of mail that piles up on the Queen's desk such as the problem letters which are always answered. For example, a crippled schoolboy wrote to the Queen explaining that six major operations had saved his life and suggesting an M.B.E. for his surgeon. The Queen saw to it that full consideration was given to the matter. A Trade Union secretary wrote to the Queen about an old stonemason thrown out of work when the restoration of the blitzed Temple Church was at last completed. "Is it possible to give him employment on Crown property?" he enquired and so, on the Queen's direct intervention, the craftsman was given a job at the Tower of London.

Mrs. Buxton, a Lincoln farm-worker's wife, was told that her six months old son, Richard, would die of a rare disease. The Queen arranged a consultation with a top London specialist who undertook the one in a million chance of a successful operation – and the boy's life was saved. "How can I ever thank you?" wrote the mother. One hears of these cases only from the people themselves for no one at the Palace discusses the Queen's correspondence.

Queen Elizabeth II has great feeling for others. Once she was watching a T.V. newsreel of herself talking to a bed-ridden woman who had been brought out of a house onto the pavement so that she would not miss the Queen as she passed. As Elizabeth watched the film, she exclaimed quite angrily: "They should never have done that. It might have killed the lady. I would have gone in to her had they asked."

The Queen has achieved much to break down colour barriers. In 1956 on the occasion of her visit to Nigeria, she appointed two Africans as her equerries – the first to enter her household.

From the start of her reign, Queen Elizabeth has worked hard for the country. For example, it was on February 3rd, 1954, that she first set foot in Australia, and during the next two months she travelled 2,500 miles by road, 900 by train, and 10,000 by plane making 35 different flights. Out of 58 days, she was to have only 6 days and 7 half days free. One intensive two-days programme it was calculated entailed her being on her feet for 20 hours.

The full list of arrangements occupied a bulky volume, which irreverently came to be known as the Black Bible, not only for the colour of its binding but also for its almost brutal demands. A statistician calculated that she made 102 speeches and listened to 200, and made 4,800 hand-shakes. She so perfected her methods of physical relaxation that she came through it all in high spirits whilst tough naval men accompanying her were worn out. After the ordeal of her first day in Sydney and enduring the noise of a million people letting it rip, when her car finally returned to Government House, she turned to her chauffeur and said: "Thank you so much, driver, this has been a trying day for you."

On average, the Queen sends 1500 letters of congratulation to centenarians a year. She will respond for diamond weddings, too. The Queen has never forgotten how when she was still a little girl she would receive correspondence from children who were lonely, all expressing affection and loyalty. She remembers how her grandmother, Queen Mary, would sit at her desk every morning at 9.00 a.m. dealing with all her correspondence personally and meticulously. Then, when as Princess Elizabeth she lived at Clarence House, it was partly staffed by applicants who wrote for jobs out of the blue.

A sixteen-year old youth named Ernest Poole poured into a letter his love of horses and his ambition to become a jockey. A job in a racing stable he pleaded could start him at the bottom of the ladder. "I know how you like horses," he ended. "You will understand how I feel." Within 48 hours he learned that his letter had been forwarded to the Queen's racing trainer at that time, Captain Boyd-Rochfort. Within a week he began work at the Captain's Newmarket stables.

When the Queen visited Nigeria in 1956 she made a point of visiting a leper colony and mixing freely with the occupants – the modern equivalent of the royal touch for the King's Evil. The supervisor of the colony commented: "This will do more to conquer man's fear of the disease than any other single act I can think of. It will convince them as nothing else could that most of their fears of the disease are groundless, for people all over the world will read about how the Queen penetrated a leper settlement." Similarly, the late Princess Diana visited those suffering from Aids, and no doubt her two sons will be influenced by her example.

Sir Winston Churchill first met Queen Elizabeth II at Balmoral when she was only two years old and wrote to his wife, Clementine, that the Princess had "an air of authority and reflectiveness astonishing in an infant".

Harold Macmillan once said that it was a pity the Queen often looked so solemn when she had such a superb sense of humour. The comment was passed on to her and when they met she said that she believed the Sovereign should look serious. Otherwise, people would not take what she said seriously if she were always grinning.

Few realise the exacting work the Queen has to do. She must keep abreast of events all over the world that might affect her country. She does not live in an ivory tower. Her powers are limited, for she reigns but she does not rule. If she herself is doubtful about anything, she can show it by asking for more information. Whilst all laws are framed in her name, they are enforced by her Ministers in accordance with the powers given them by the electorate.

She is the epitome of tact whilst Prince Philip has spent his life being controversial. On one occasion when several people were present and the conversation became politically sensitive, Philip asked for her opinion. She immediately looked under the table where her corgis often hide at mealtime and she called: "Sugar, Sugar where are you, Sugar?"

Relating this episode, Philip commented dryly: "That is Lillibet's defence mechanism coming into play. If she doesn't want to commit herself she calls the dogs!"

When the Queen was crowned in 1953 it was with St. Edward's Crown, the official Crown of England. This weighed 2.25 kg and was much heavier than the Imperial State Crown that the Queen wore after the ceremony and has worn at all subsequent State Openings of Parliament. To get used to the heavier St. Edward's Crown, the Queen wore it around Buckingham Palace beforehand, even when feeding her corgis.

Prince Charles, like his mother, is always careful that no one around him should be embarrassed. At a dinner when a Third World leader was the guest of honour and began to drink the water from his finger bowl, the Prince did the same. He once left a note for his secretary asking him to get the chef to have ready by 5p.m. two large tubes of custard which he was going to take to a party at an old friend Lady Sarah Keswick's house. Naturally, the chef assumed it was for eating and prepared a superb custard. The Prince is Godfather to one of her children and it was for the birthday celebrations. The Prince took the tubes with him in the back of his car, for they were intended for throwing not eating – and when the custard had cooled it made the most appalling mess. Lady Keswick's father, the Queen Mother's Treasurer, was furious, for his dining-room had to be entirely redecorated.

Like her mother, the Queen never misses church on Sunday. Prince Charles was once spending the week-end with friends who asked him if he wanted to attend a local church or go fishing. He chose to fish, saying: "I can pray when I am fishing but I cannot fish in church."

Attending church is not obligatory if one is staying with the Queen, but she prefers her guests to make the effort. She must believe that cleanliness is next to Godliness because some of her guests leave far cleaner than when they arrive – especially if they have been staying elsewhere first. Should they arrive with dirty laundry, it will be immediately whisked away and returned impeccably washed and ironed. The men's guns will have been cleaned and a brace of birds, boxed for travelling, will have been added to their luggage. It is not good manners to arrive at any of the Royal Homes in a car that looks as if it has been driven through a mud-bath. People do, yet they will drive away in a vehicle that is immaculate and polished.

When the Queen holds at Buckingham Palace a "Meet the People Luncheon", guests are specially selected from jockeys to journalists, actresses to artists, and so on. This was introduced after the Queen discontinued the annual presentation of débutantes at Court in July 1958, when it was also announced that she intended to create her son Charles, Prince of Wales.

The Queen's face is normally impassive, except at race meetings. Then, she can look as disappointed as anyone with a pound each way bet when her horse loses and as delighted as a child when she wins. Her own judgment of form is astonishingly good, like that of the Queen Mother.

Prince Philip was born on the 10th of June 1921, in a villa owned by his parents on the island of Corfu. He was the youngest of five and the only boy. His father was Prince Andrew of Greece and his English-born mother was the beautiful Princess Alice of Battenburg, daughter of the first Marquis of Milford Haven and sister of Lord Louis Mountbatten. They drifted apart and Philip grew up to be an extrovert little boy whose life was an endless round of visits to royal relatives. It was his mother's elder brother George, the Marquis of Milford Haven, who eventually gave the eight-year old a home in England and paid for him to go to Cheam School and then eventually to the new school which Hahn had opened at Gordonstoun in Scotland, and where Philip was happy thriving under a régime which put more importance on self-reliance and fitness than academic qualifications. When he left, he was Captain of Cricket and Hockey, and his seamanship had earned him the rare privilege of sailing an open boat in the Moray Firth without adult supervision.

When Uncle George died in 1938, Lord Mountbatten took over the responsibility for the 17-year old Philip and used his influence to ensure that the youth passed the entrance examination for Dartmouth and arranged a crammer course to fill the gaps in Hahn's system of education. He organised his nephew's life, and began to wonder if perhaps it would be possible to marry him to the future Queen of England.

It was in 1939 at Dartmouth when Philip first met the 13-year old Princess Elizabeth. Weary from being made to dig a trench, he half-heartedly showed her and Margaret how to operate a model train at the home of the future Admiral Frederick Dalrymple-Hamilton, then in charge at Dartmouth. For Elizabeth, Philip was Prince Charming with his athletic bearing, his chiselled face, freshness and wholesomeness. From then, he became the only man she loved or would ever love.

A few weeks after this meeting, war broke out and Philip's plans to only train for the Royal Navy and then leave the service were abandoned, and he was enlisted, passing out of Dartmouth as a special entry cadet and winner of the King's Dirk. Louis Mountbatten arranged his first posting which was on HMS *Ramilles*. He went aboard on 24th February 1940 in Colombo. Later he was to confide to his commander: "My uncle has ideas for me – he thinks I should marry Princess Elizabeth." He was asked whether he was fond of her, and replied: "Oh, yes, I write to her every week."

In the Sub-Lieutenant's examination, Prince Philip came through in January, 1941, with four Firsts and one Second. This meant that he went back to sea in the old destroyer, *Wallace*, with nine months' seniority out of a possible ten, and when he became her First Lieutenant in October, 1942, at the request of his own Captain, who knew a good thing when he saw one, Philip at the age of 21 was one of the youngest seconds-in-command in the Royal Navy. Now he was kept busy on East Coast convoy work among bombs and torpedoes. He was determined that the *Wallace* should be run better than any other destroyer in the Squadron. He knew by name all in the ship's company of 250 men.

After serving in the *Wallace*, Philip became second-in-command of *Whelp* with the 27th Destroyer Flotilla in the Pacific and up against the Japanese off Burma and Sumatra and poised for the invasion of Japan when the bomb fell on Hiroshima. When in July, 1951, he quit the Royal Navy he was commanding the frigate *Magpie*. By the War's end, he had sailed over every ocean, covered the evacuations of Greece and Crete, the Canadian landings in Sicily, the Allied invasions of North Africa, and had survived many battles.

In May, 1948, Princess Elizabeth had been a bridesmaid to her own lady-in-waiting, the Honourable Mrs Vicary Gibbs. At the reception afterwards at the Savoy Hotel, Prince Philip was present and they were seen together at other social events. In June, the Commandos gave a ball at which Princess Elizabeth was guest of honour. Then that summer the Prince joined the Royal Family at Balmoral and at some time during the holiday he proposed marriage. A wedding would have to wait until he could be naturalised, but Elizabeth accepted immediately. He was then serving as an instructor at the Petty Officers' School at Corsham in Wiltshire. With the King and Queen about to leave on a tour of South Africa, it was decided to keep a public announcement secret. In early September, Buckingham Palace issued a statement denying the media speculation of an engagement.

On Saturday, 1st February, 1947, the King and Queen accompanied by the two Princesses, sailed in the new battleship HMS *Vanguard*. The passage was rough and the vessel was damaged in the Bay of Biscay. On the 17th they arrived at Cape Town to a delighted welcome. The Union Parliament was opened by the King on the 21st and Princess Elizabeth named a dock after her on 3rd March. During the royal party's visit to the National Park in

Natal, it was announced that Prince Philip, following renunciation of his foreign titles, had been granted British citizenship and would in future be known as Lieutenant Philip Mountbatten, R.N. On Monday 21st April, Princess Elizabeth celebrated her 21st birthday during the South African tour and broadcast to her homeland: "There is a motto which has been borne by many of my ancestors – a noble motto – I serve. Those words were an inspiration to many bygone heirs to the throne and they would also be the same to me."

Since his marriage to the Queen in November 1947 Prince Philip has found his energies best employed outside Buckingham Palace. He has involved himself in education, conservation, science, medicine, sport, wild life and industry; and has never steered away from controversy when, in his opinion, something needs to be said. He jokingly refers to his personal style as 'dontopedalogy' – the science of opening your mouth and putting your foot in.

Philip is clearly strong-willed and a firm influence on his family but in public, when accompanying the Queen on official duties, he goes to great lengths to demonstrate that he is very much playing the role of Consort. He is concerned nowadays with over 400 separate organisations, and makes on average about 90 speeches a year, all of which he writes personally. He enjoys wild life photography, but also likes shooting as a sport. He reconciles the conflict which arises from this by pointing out that far more wild life perishes by insecticide than the gun, but at the same time he is violently opposed to all that might endanger the survival of a species. His arguments and attitudes are very much those of a countryman. He understands forestry and agriculture. There has been something of a renaissance for example, at Balmoral. In 1955 he introduced Highland cattle and, in 1966, a herd of Luing cattle, shorthorns crossed with Highland. In 1972 he purchased a herd of Galloways. In order to get the best out of what is in effect a small estate he has introduced the very latest methods of agricultural technology.

In 1956 Prince Philip inaugurated the Duke of Edinburgh's Award Scheme, providing a challenge for young people to reach certain standards in their activities outside their schools or jobs. Four hundred types of activity qualify for entry and the scheme became enormously popular throughout not only the United Kingdom but also the Commonwealth. Those who are awarded the highest recognition, the gold medal, are invited to Buckingham Palace to meet the Prince, who is always ready to go anywhere to give rallying speeches in support of any cause he believes in. Whatever the cause, he is never daunted, such as when a business man offered him a cheque for £100,000 for a favoured cause of his and threw the cheque into the river. Philip at once whipped off his jacket and diving in brought back the prized piece of paper, between his teeth.

Always athletic and competitive, Prince Philip has headed the Central Council for Physical Recreation, and the London Federation of Boys' Clubs. For over 20 years he was President of the International Equestrian Federation. He has been President of the MCC. He might have played more cricket were it not for the Queen and his Uncle, Lord Mountbatten. He has said: "I made a serious mistake of underestimating my wife's interest in horses." When as Princess Elizabeth, she came out to Malta 1949 and was offered the choice of watching her husband play cricket or Mountbatten play polo she always opted for the polo. Philip realised that if he was going to see anything of her he would have to accept his uncle's offer to teach him and provide him with ponies. And so began a long love affair with the game. In later life, his favourite sport has become carriage driving. In 1973 he entered the second ever European Championship driving the famous Balmoral 'dogcart'. Carriage-driving has extended his interest in design and technology. The early carriages were antique vehicles not suited to the rigours of competition driving.

The Duke concluded that an all-metal carriage using a proper steel frame was the answer. Philip is definitely a sporting prince and much of his life has been spent falling off horses and carriages and boats. As Tim Heald has written in his biography of the Duke of Edinburgh "to the office-bound and the sedentary, these pre-occupations of the Duke may seem incomprehensible, and even frivolous. He, on the other hand, would find a life divided – like so many other people's – between the desk and the T.V. impossible to contemplate."

The Duke of Edinburgh loves to sail in racing ships. When Prince Charles and Princess Anne were teenagers he took them sailing in Scottish lochs and at one time, with the ocean-going yawl, *Bloodhound*, they made a thorough exploration of the west coast. Polo and carriage driving are other pastimes. The former, however, he gave up in 1971 after a wrist injury. The latter he took up with considerable energy as a result, and he is often to be found at championships in Scotland such as take place at Scone Palace or at Mellerstain, near Kelso in the Borders, the home of Lord Binning. Unlike the Queen, however, he shows little interest in racing or breeding horses.

Another hobby is painting, at which he is quite accomplished. He prefers landscapes although he occasionally tackles figures and still life. He is modest about his talent – "I don't claim any exceptional interest or knowledge or ability," he says. "It's strictly average." But he took lessons from the artist Edward Seago, and often visits exhibitions such as the annual Royal Scottish Academy summer show in Edinburgh. He is quite prepared to speak his mind on the subject of modern art, although he is equally enthusiastic when he recognises real ability. Through a meeting in 1948 with the painter, George Halliday, and Gordon Russell, the Duke took steps to encourage the pursuit of good design and from this came about the Design Centre and an annual award for good design at work.

Foremost, Philip is his own man, sensitive to the expectations of his role in the Royal Family, both in public and in private. "I am not a graduate of any university," he once told a conference of academics. "I am not a humanist or a scientist, and oddly enough I don't regret it. I owe my allegiance to another of the world's few really great fraternities, that of the sea. There one will find all the conflicts that man has had to contend with now and in the past: the fear of the unknown, the power that is greater than man and his machines, the necessity to reconcile human frailties to scientific gadgets."

Prince Philip has proved himself to be a witty and observant speaker. For example, he said: "You can't go through life like a man in a rowing-boat. He may get a splendid view of where he's been, but unless he looks over his shoulders every now and then, he's likely to get into a nasty muddle. The ideal man is healthy and fit and has a well-trained mind. The bookworm and the gladiator are only half-trained men leading only half a life. Untrained intelligence is as much use as a bottle opener without an opener. You can't train a boy to be a king – but if you train him to be a man then he can be anything. I always feel the speeches should be over before the last speaker is rendered completely invisible by the accumulated cigar smoke."

Opening a dental hospital, the Prince said: "Anyone who has ever suffered at the hands of a dentist will be happy that this place will help the training of dentists. I declare it – wide open." About Karl Marx, he observed: "A man can be forgiven a lot if he can quote Shakespeare in an economic treatise." Speaking to the Institute of Personnel Managers he feared that, "if anyone had a new idea there were twice as many people who advocated putting a man with a red flag in front of it. The trouble with senior management to an outsider is that there are too many one-ulcer men holding down two-ulcer men's jobs.

"Frankly, I would like to see the day when a person's work may decide their income, but where their leisure activity and voluntary work decides their social standing... It's no good shutting your eyes and saying 'Britain is Best' three times a day after meals, and expecting it to be so."

Prince Philip often goes out of his way to help people who write to him. On August 9th, 1963, he received a letter from a Mrs. Martin, all about 'Dad's book' which nobody would publish. 'Dad' was in fact her father-in-law, a retired clergyman of 86 who most of his life had spent painting wild flowers. She enclosed many of the rejection letters. "I did wonder," she ended, "if you could suggest any way we could try to get the book published." The Prince wrote back asking Mrs. Martin to send him one or two reproductions. Philip then set about trying to get the book published himself. All publishers he tried said the same – cost would be great and sales small. After eighteen months, John Hadfield of George Rainbird found a way of publishing it in association with the National Magazine Company and Michael Joseph. The book came out the following summer illustrated with some 1,400 exquisite paintings, title: *A Concise British Flora* by W. Keble Martin, and became a best seller, soon exhausting its first printing of 50,000 copies and two more of 25,000 each. Prince Philip wrote the Foreword and bought 24 copies.

Prince Philip as President of the National Playing Fields Association from 1949 to 1972 has worked valiantly, to quote his own words at the outset, "squeezing all the rich people I know for all the juice I can get out of them" and prodding the authorities to buy derelict land for recreational purposes and stressing: "You may believe that you have designed the perfect playing field as seen through adult eyes, but I can assure you that it may prove deadly dull to a child of four."

As a result of Prince Philip's endeavours, by 1953 some 200 playing fields a year were being opened by him. He set up the

Maritime Trust and became concerned with the preservation of historic hulks often falling apart in remote anchorages and which once lost would leave no other examples of the kind of ships existing in earlier times. He wrote to Sir Solly Zuckerman, then scientific adviser to the Cabinet, asking for a grant. He got a gloomy reply and an alternative suggestion: "Why not model ships instead?" He wrote back to Solly who was Hon. Sec. of the Zoo also: "I take your points about models. How would you react to the suggestion that the Zoo could be run more cheaply if all the exhibits were stuffed animals?"

Prince Charles won a B.A. Honours Degree at Trinity College, Cambridge, and spent some months at Aberystwyth learning Welsh preparing for his investiture as the 21st Prince of Wales in a ceremony at Caernarvon Castle in 1969. Two years later, he enlisted at R.A.F. Cranwell, followed by time at Dartmouth's Royal Naval College and on vessels at sea.

In 1966, Prince Charles spent a year in Australia at Timbertop. Since then he has described that year as "the most wonderful experience of my life". He has always been keen to undertake new experiences such as diving under the Arctic ice.

As well as serving in the R.A.F. and the Royal Navy, Prince Charles has kept up his connections with the Army as part of his public duties and private pastimes. For example, in January 1975 when training with the Royal Marines Centre at Lympstone, Devon, he successfully accomplished tasks such as wading down a stream, crawling through half-submerged pipes, and tree-walking. The following year, he trained with the Parachute Regiment of which he is Colonel-in-Chief. He was taught to play polo, by his uncle, Lord Mountbatten, at which he excelled, but when he started having a number of serious accidents he was forbidden by the Queen to continue playing. His other passion is opera and he is President of the Friends of Covent Garden.

On 17th June 1981 he flew to New York to attend a Gala Performance of *The Sleeping Beauty* at the Metropolitan Opera House to celebrate the Royal Ballet's 50th Anniversary. This was followed by a Ball.

Also in 1981, Prince Charles received the British Book Award as 'Author of the Year' for his best selling book of the television programme on architecture, *A Vision of Britain*. He also wrote a highly successful children's book, *The Old Man of Lochnagar*. Interviewed on 3rd June 1990, he said: "I'm very busy and don't have a great deal of time for reading... But I read what I can – all kinds of this and that to keep up with things." At the Society of Authors's awards on 29th May, 1990, he spoke feelingly about the writer's problems of revealing his innermost feelings to the world. "Where may I ask you is the Monarchy going, when Princes and pressmen are in the same Boeing?"

Spurred on by his father, Prince Philip, Charles had pursued the training programme to which he realised he must devote himself as heir to the throne. In time out from his studies at Trinity, he learned to fly, then served in the Royal Air Force, majoring on Jets and winning his 'wings'. It is well-known that he was unhappy as a boarder at Gordonstoun. The question was how to solve the problem without casting a reflection on the school. Sir Robert Menzies on a visit from Australia discussed the matter with the Queen at Balmoral and suggested a solution, that Charles might spend some months at Timbertop, a branch of the Geelong Church of England Grammar School, an isolated outpost where his school mates addressed him on arrival as: "You pommy bastard!" Charles took it well and by the time he left he was the most popular boy there – and his popularity was to spread throughout Australia and contribute towards the Dominion voting against becoming a Republic. When Prince Philip met his son at the Commonwealth Games in Jamaica in 1966, he was delighted to find how sturdy he had become and at receiving a hearty bone-crushing handshake copied from the young Aussies with whom he had been mixing.

On his desk at Kensington Palace when he was living there just after his marriage, Prince Charles kept a photograph of the Duke of Edinburgh and himself dressed in Trinity House, the Lighthouse Institution Uniform, with the Prince a step behind his father. On the photograph Charles has written: "I was not made to follow in my father's footsteps." The Prince has not the temperament to do so, though he has always tried to live up to everything his father expected of him. He is not by nature competitive nor is he aggressive. Charles is both sensitive and thoughtful. Prince Philip himself has said: "Charles has his mother's serenity and concern for individuals, but also her unsuspected inner toughness."

In 1997 the Director of the Prince's Trust wrote: "The Monarchy is moving from being an institution principally famous for ceremonial occasions to one of value for what it can do for the country through public service."

The *Big Issue*, the voice of the homeless and dispossessed, elected Prince Charles "Hero of the Year" in 1999. The Prince is indeed conducting his life true to his motto '*Ich dien*'.

Prince Charles's *Youth Business Trust* is the largest business agency in the country and created 39,000 companies and 52,000 jobs as reported in *The Times* for 27th December 1996. James Morton in his book, *Breaking the Cycle*, published in 1998, states that Prince Charles believes that social problems are best remedied by local initiative and self-help. Of those opinions sampled in a Mori poll of June 1999, 85 per cent thought him 'caring'. His advisers believe, according to Frank Prochaska in *The Republic of Britain*, that he will succeed in persuading the public that he is "a conscientious King (or hereditary president?) in waiting".

In his brilliant book, Prochaska states that one of the arguments in favour of retaining a monarchy in the nineteenth century was that by propping up so many voluntary societies it acted as a defender of institutional democracy. In so doing, it served as a buffer between the state and society and acted as a counterweight to the dictatorial tendencies of central government. Prochaska continues that the present Queen endorsed such views in her 1991 Christmas broadcast on charitable service and a free society. As she saw it, a healthy voluntary sector, independent of government control was the foundation of an open society. "Democracy depends not on political structures, but on the goodwill and the sense of responsibility of each and every citizen."

Frank Prochaska discerningly comments: "As so much of the Crown's mystery has been dissipated by royal scrapes and tabloid intrusion, it is likely that the monarchy will be judged increasingly on the practical benefits it brings to society."

The adjective that covers all Prince Charles's beliefs in how the country should be run is indeed 'CARING'. In his leaflet, entitled: 'Working Together' are described the aims of what he calls his family of organisations whose common purpose is to help the disadvantaged and the adventurous through grants, loans or training. He is in charge of no less than six Trusts and has built an Annexe to his country home at Highgrove where those who have come to consult him, some in their wheel-chairs, can stay. After opening his Shelter for the Homeless in South London during the severe winter of 2001, Prince Charles was interviewed by B.B.C. Television on the occasion of the 25th anniversary of his Prince's Trust. He said that witnessing the sorry plight of people in Birmingham had made him want to do something practical to help them. It had begun with one or two people and was now so huge that it employed over 4,000 and a huge army of volunteers. He now spends his life writing letters to raise money and to thank people for their donations.

His sister, Princess Anne, regularly visits Africa taking part in the perilous work of helping to clear land mines in the war zones.

In late July 2001, Prince Charles launched the *Business in the Community*'s Rural Action Programme – a new initiative to encourage companies to use their immense power for good to help rural communities. It was a call for action to all those businesses which care about what happens to 90 per cent of the land mass of Britain and those who live and work in it. He said that nearly 20 years ago he became President of *Business in the Community* because he was growing increasingly concerned about the desperate situation facing so many inner cities. It was the time of the riots in Brixton and Toxteth when, to a large extent, it seemed that the wider community had decided that these problems were someone else's responsibility. "I believed they were the responsibility of each and every one of us – not least the business community. Since that time *Business in the Community* has rightly focused its attention on the inner cities – and the companies which have been a part of this have helped to bring real relief to some of the most deprived areas of the country."

But in recent years even before the foot-and-mouth outbreak, agricultural returns and farm employment were at their lowest since the 1930's. Average farm incomes were now £5,200 per farm. Rural pubs had been closing at the rate of six a week and more than 40 per cent of parishes had no permanent shop of any kind and 43 per cent no post office. In the year 2000 alone 20,000 jobs were lost in agriculture.

Nevertheless, within rural communities there was a remarkable resolve to create new businesses suited to the new world in which people found themselves. Women have been showing particularly resourcefulness and enterprise. The potential for business leaders to encourage this spirit of determination is great. That was why over the past eight months, he had led four "Seeing is Believing" visits to rural areas, taking business leaders to see for themselves the problems that exist. On each occasion the business leaders admitted that they had not understood the extent or the urgency of the difficulties, or known how they could help, until they had seen them first-hand.

So what role can business play in the countryside – and why should it get involved? The reasons were not simply economic, although such reasons clearly did exist: many companies have significant operations and sales, or draw staff from rural areas, and the food industry takes much of its raw materials from the countryside. For these companies, rural decline can mean business decline. But even if a company does not have a direct commercial connection, all businesses have a wider social responsibility. That was why the Rural Action launch proposed practical action in four key areas.

Prince Charles gave as his campaign's first initiative was to encourage businesses and the community to buy their food locally. There were huge environmental and economic advantages to eating what is produced locally rather than importing goods from hundreds, and sometimes thousands, of mile away. "Imagine what a difference it would make if every hotel, in-house canteen and supermarket tried to buy its food first from local producers." The Prince went on to give examples of firms that were already putting these proposals of his into action. "This sort of local sourcing should become the norm rather than the exception. That is why *Business in the Community* is working with the Institute of Grocery Distribution to develop case studies of best practice and to demonstrate that local sourcing can provide a competitive advantage."

The Prince believes that the second action area is for business to help with the provision of rural services – without which no community can survive, let alone flourish. We cannot turn the clock back, so we must be imaginative about finding alternatives to old ways. For instance, with village shops, post offices and banks closing at an alarming rate, he wants to see if we can make the "Pub the Hub" by encouraging landlords to take on some of these services in the pub itself.

The revival of market towns, which for centuries have been important as centres of rural economic activity but are now in decline, is the Prince's third initiative. *Business in the Community Rural Action* already has a pilot scheme in Yorkshire, supported financially by the *Countryside Agency* and *RDA Yorkshire Forward*, to bring forward professional business skills to rebrand and manage market towns so that they can attract businesses and become engines for regional economic enterprise. With the active help of businesses, BITC wants "to roll this out nationally".

And, finally, business needs to support the community entrepreneur. If there was one thing Prince Charles had learnt over the years, it is that imposing solutions on any community from on high achieves little more than resentment. There are already thousands of individuals around the country giving leadership in their own communities. All they need is help, advice and maybe a little financial support.

For instance, in the village of Orton in Cumbria, a farmers' market had made the difference between success and failure for a number of local producers. When one of the organisers, Jane Brook, was struggling to set it up, what she needed above all was advice on how to overcome bureaucracy, as well as some marketing help. Having heard of Jane's experiences on one of the Prince's *Seeing is Believing* visits, *The Co-operative Group* is now generously leading a *Partners in Rural Leadership* programme which will bring together an initial 50 rural entrepreneurs with 50 leading business managers in order to share ideas and offer advice.

On top of this, said the Prince, *The Co-operative Group* is providing access to computer services and online networks. And as an extension to this, *Business in the Community* is partnering Harper Adams College to expand their *Women in Rural Enterprise* scheme nationwide, specifically to help women to start businesses or diversify. HSBC is providing a package of finance and business support, including softer loans and training its branch managers to ensure that they better understand the problems that women entrepreneurs might be facing.

From the business leaders with whom Prince Charles is already working on the *Rural Action* initiative, he claimed that he knew there was a determination and a goodwill to act. From the pilot schemes that they were already operating, they knew what a difference corporate involvement can make. Business must not underestimate the power that it has, with its unique resources and skills, to help to keep alive communities in our countryside.

There had been much talk during the foot-and-mouth outbreak of the long-term consequences of slaughtering so-called "hefted" flocks of sheep. These are sheep which, through generations of breeding, have come to know their territory intimately and have adapted to the particular conditions of their habitat. Likewise, if that link between the farming communities and their land which has been built up over generations is severed, we will have lost something precious which cannot be reinvested. We simply must find a way to ensure that people born and bred in the countryside, and who want to stay there, can find an economic future, be that on the family farm or running their own business.

Prince Charles ended that the British countryside is only as beautiful as it is because it has been cared for, and lived in, by these people with generations of experience and knowledge. The unique scenery, and the people who live amongst it, are one of this country's most treasured national assets. "They are also a crucial economic resource, with so much income coming from tourism. It has never been more threatened than it is today and the opportunities for business to make a real and lasting impact have never been greater. With your help, *Business in the Community* can make a substantial difference."

King George III, known as 'Farmer' George, Prince Charles's ancestor, would have applauded such a speech.

Bibliography

Airlie, Mabell, Countess of, *Thatched With Gold, The Memoirs of Mabell, Countess of Airlie*, Hutchinson, 1962.

Alice, Princess of Great Britain, *For My Grandchildren*, Evans Bros., 1966.

Arthur, Sir George Compton Archiband, *Queen Alexandra*, Chapman & Hall, 1934.

Arthur George, *King George V*, Jonathan Cape, 1939.

Bagehot, Walter, *The English Constitution*, 1867.

Battiscombe, Georgina, *Queen Alexandra*, Constable, 1969.

Beaton, Cecil, *The Wandering Years*, Weidenfeld and Nicolson, 1961.

Black, Percy, *The Mystique of Modern Monarchy*, Watts, 1953.

Bolitho, Hector, *Edward VIII, His Life and Reign*, Eyre and Spottiswoode, 1937.

Bolitho, Hector, *King George VI*, Lippincott, 1938.

Boothroyd, J. Basil, *Philip, an Informal Biography*, Longman, 1971.

Bradford, Sarah, *King George VI*, Weidenfeld & Nicolson, 1979.

Brook-Shepherd, Gordon, *Uncle of Europe: The Social and Diplomatic Life of Edward VII*, Collins, 1975.

Bryant, Arthur, *George V*, Peter Davies, 1936.

Bryant, Arthur, *A Thousand Years of British Monarchy*, Collins, 1975.

Cathcart, Helen, *The Queen Mother Herself*, W.H. Allen, 1979.

Channon, Sir Henry, *Chips, The Diaries of Sir Henry Channon*, edited by Robert Rhodes James, Weidenfeld and Nicolson, 1967.

Churchill, Sir Winston S., *The Second World War*, 6 vols. 1948-54.

Cooke, Kinloch, *Pss. Mary Adelaide, Dss. Of Teck*, Vol. I and Vol. II, John Murray, 1900.

Corby, Tom, MVO, *Her Majesty, Queen Elizabeth, the Queen Mother*, Berkeley House Publishing Ltd., 2000.

Crawford, Marian, *The Little Princesses*, Cassell, 1950.

Dennis, Geoffrey, *Coronation Commentary*, Heinemann, 1937.

Hibbert, Christopher, *Edward VII: A Portrait*, Allen Lane, 1976.

Hibbert, Christopher, *The Court of St. James, The Monarch at Work from Victoria to Elizabeth II*, Weidenfeld and Nicolson, 1979.

Longford, Elizabeth, *Royal Throne – The Future of the Monarchy*, Weidenfeld & Nicolson, 1979.

Magnus, Sir Philip Montefiore, *King Edward the Seventh*, John Murray, 1964.

Mountbatten, Earl, *Mountbatten. Eighty Years in Pictures*, Macmillan, 1979.

Nicolson, Harold, *King George V, His Life and Reign*, Constable, 1952.

Plumb, J.H. and Wheldon, Huw, *Royal Heritage, The Treasures of the British Crown*, Harcourt Brace Jovanovich, 1977.

Ponsonby, Sir Frederick, *Recollections of Three Reigns*, Eyre and Spottiswoode, 1951.

Pope-Hennessy, James, *Queen Mary, 1867-1953*, Allen & Unwin, 1959.

Queen Mary's Doll's House, Pitkin Pictorials, 1978.

St. Aubyn, Giles, *Edward VII Prince and King*, William Collins Ltd., 1970.

Victoria, Queen, *Further Letters of Queen Victoria From the Archives of Brandenburg-Prussia*, translated by Mrs. J. Pudney and Lord Sudley and edited by Hector Bolitho, Butterworth, 1938.

Victoria, Queen, *Dearest Child: Letters Between Queen Victoria and the Princess Royal, 1858-1961*, edited by Roger Fulford, Evans Bros., 1964.

Wheeler-Bennett, John W., *King George VI – His Life and Reign*, Macmillan, 1958.

Williams, Neville, *Chronology of the Modern World 1763-1965*, Barrie & Rockliff, 1966.

ALSO FROM SHEPHEARD-WALWYN

The Royal Law
The Source of our Freedom Today
L.L. Blake

'The richness of thought and quotation contained in this small volume ...
make it a study that anyone with claims to hold intelligent views on
government and monarchy, cannot possibly afford to ignore'
CHURCH OF ENGLAND NEWSPAPER

Although people are aware of the marvellous sense of history and
pomp surrounding the coronation of a British monarch, very few appreci-
ate that the words of the coronation have a strong bearing upon our civil
liberties. This concise yet authoritative analysis highlights the constitutional importance of the coronation, emphasising that it is not simply a
red-robed and ermine-trimmed pageant, but an important acknowledge-
ment of Divine Law which forms the source of all law within our country.

The author considers the lasting impact of the statement made by the
13th century lawyer, Bracton, that the monarch 'must not be under man
but under God and the law, for the law makes the king'. Indeed, it is
this principle which led to King John signing the Magna Carta in 1215.
Bracton's statement still influences our civil freedoms today and
regulates the work of public servants from prime minister to police
officer. It has given rise to the concept of freedom under law which has
spread to large parts of the world today.

Two appendices contain large parts of the coronation service of
Elizabeth II and an Anglo-Saxon document on government attributed to
Wulfstan, Archbishop of York.

'Occasionally one comes upon a book that one would like to make many
other people read ...such a book is The Royal Law ...'
CATHOLIC HERALD

'This whole book deserves the highest praise ...'
PRAYER BOOK SOCIETY

210 X 148mm 128pp index ISBN 0 85683 191 3 **£12.95 hardback**

The Prince and the Professor

A Dialogue on the Place of the Monarchy in the 21st Century

L.L. Blake

with line drawings by Barrington Barber

'The author should be applauded for raising the debate about the purpose of monarchy to an intelligent level.' FINANCIAL TIMES

This wide-ranging conversation between a fictional young prince and an old professor of constitutional law covers sovereignty; the pros and cons of a republic; Plato on freedom and democracy; the role of the press; and the notion of contract underlying modern written constitutions compared with the medieval concept of status found in the British constitution.

The professor accepts the need for change but warns against changes forced through by politicians who misjudge their effects. He explains the monarch's role, looking to the long-term welfare of the nation, above party politics and acting as a unifying factor in the national life.

229 x 145mm   128pp   ISBN 0 85683 165 4   **£9.95 paperback**

Royal Families Worldwide

Mark Watson

'I have little doubt that anyone interested in royalty who buys this book will constantly be referring to it on matters of modern detail.'
PAUL MINET, ROYALTY DIGEST

This handy up-to-date reference work on 50 royal families around the world includes a short introduction on the role of modern monarchy. The arrangement is alphabetical by country and some non-regnant families are also listed.

To facilitate comparison between countries information is summarised under set headings: monarch/head of the family; date and place of birth; parentage; siblings; religion; date of marriage; consort(s); children; residence; date of succession; constitutional status; source of income; and brief history of the dynasty. On the facing page is a photograph of the monarch/head of family.

214 x 136mm   ISBN 0 85683 170 0 **£18.95 hardback**